Alpha Mathematics 2

New Edition

Compiled by

T. R. Goddard,

J. W. Adams and R. P. Beaumont

 Schofield & Sims Ltd Huddersfield

0 7217 2251 2

First printed 1979

Reprinted 1979

Reprinted 1980

Reprinted 1981

Reprinted 1982

Reprinted 1983

Revised and reprinted 1987

Reprinted 1989

The books in the two series forming this programme comprise:

Ready for Alpha and Beta 0 7217 2266 0

Beta Mathematics 1 0 7217 2258 X	Alpha Mathematics 1 0 7217 2250 4
Beta Mathematics 2 0 7217 2259 8	Alpha Mathematics 2 0 7217 2251 2
Beta Mathematics 3 0 7217 2260 1	Alpha Mathematics 3 0 7217 2252 0
Beta Mathematics 4 0 7217 2261 X	Alpha Mathematics 4 0 7217 2253 9
Beta Mathematics 5 0 7217 2268 7	
Beta Mathematics 6 0 7217 2269 5	

Designed by Peter Sinclair (Design and Print) Ltd, Wetherby

Printed in England by Chorley & Pickersgill Ltd, Leeds

Contents   Alpha Mathematics 2

Decimal number system

A Draw this table on squared paper and write in these numbers.
Make sure that each figure is in the correct column.

	H	T	U
1			
2			
3			

1 two hundred 2 nine hundred and fifty 3 six hundred and two

> **Remember** The value of each figure is given by its **place** or **position**.

B Draw and complete these tables on squared paper.

1

Th	H	T	U

←— **10×** —→

Th	H	T	U
			1
		1	0
	1	0	0

2

Th	H	T	U
		1	0
	1	0	0
1	0	0	0

—— **÷10** —→

Th	H	T	U

What have you discovered when a number is moved:

3 one place to the left

4 one place to the right?

5 Draw and complete these tables on squared paper.

Th	H	T	U

←— **10×** —→

Th	H	T	U
			5
		7	6
		8	0
	1	4	6
	3	9	0

6

Th	H	T	U
		4	0
	3	5	0
	6	0	0
1	2	8	0
2	3	0	0

—— **÷10** —→

Th	H	T	U

C Look carefully at the tables below.
You have found that when a figure is moved:

a one place to the **left** it becomes 10 times **larger**

b one place to the **right** it becomes 10 times **smaller**.

Look at the tables below.

1 What happens to the 1 in the units column when it is moved one place to the right?

Th	H	T	U
1	0	0	0
	1	0	0
		1	0
			1

—÷10→

Th	H	T	U	tenths
	1	0	0	
		1	0	
			1	
				1

Draw and complete the tables below.

2

T	U	tenths
	4	
	8	
1	5	

—— **÷10** —→

T	U	tenths

3

T	U	tenths

←— **10×** —

T	U	tenths
		6
3	7	
2	9	

Draw this table and write in these numbers.

H	T	U	tenths

4 $\frac{9}{10}$ 5 $2\frac{3}{10}$ 6 $10\frac{9}{10}$

7 $100\frac{1}{10}$ 8 116   9 $205\frac{5}{10}$

Decimal number system

A In the decimal number system, **tenths** are written as **decimal fractions**.

The **decimal point** separates the **whole ones** from the **parts** of a whole one.

> **Example**
> 2 whole ones and 3 tenths or $2\frac{3}{10}$
> is written 2.3 (read as '2 point 3').

Write as decimal fractions:
1. 3 whole ones and 4 tenths
2. 5 whole ones and 9 tenths
3. 0 whole ones and 6 tenths
4. 8 whole ones and 8 tenths
5. 7 whole ones and 3 tenths
6. $2\frac{5}{10}$ 7. $10\frac{7}{10}$ 8. $11\frac{1}{10}$ 9. $100\frac{2}{10}$.

Write the numbers in the table below in words and then read them to your partner who will check them from the answer book. The first one is done for you.

10. eighteen point three

Hundreds	Tens	Units	tenths
		1	8	3
11		2	0	4
12	3	0	6	9
13			7	6
14	4	7	0	8
15		5	5	5

Write the numbers shown in the pictures below, using a decimal point. The first one is done for you.

16. 42.1
17.
18.
19.
20.
21.
22.

B Write the number shown on each abacus picture in figures and then in words.

1. 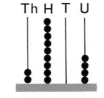 2.

3. 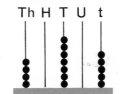 4.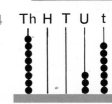

Draw abacus pictures to show these numbers.
5. five thousand and seventy
6. three thousand and fifty-two
7. one thousand and eight point five
8. two thousand and twenty-seven point one
9. one thousand, one hundred and ten point eight

C Write the value of the figure underlined in each of these numbers.
1. 7003 2. 15.8 3. 9430
4. 208.2 5. 480.7 6. 614.6
7. 1876.4 8. 1300.5 9. 111.1

Complete the following.
The first one is done for you.
10. 93 units = 9 tens 3 units
11. 47 tens = ☐hundreds ☐tens
12. 59 hundreds = ☐thousands ☐hundreds
13. 59 hundreds = ☐tens = ☐units
14. 837 = ☐tens ☐units = ☐hundreds ☐units
15. 5342 = ☐hundreds ☐tens ☐units
16. 6020 = ☐hundreds ☐tens

How many units are there in:
17. 100.2 18. 152.6 19. 11.1 20. 103.3?

How many tens are there in:
21. 74 22. 356 23. 154.9 24. 1050.7?

How many tenths are there in:
25. 3.8 26. 1.0 27. 1.5 28. 17.6?

Decimal number system

A Write as a decimal the sum of:

1. 3 tenths and 5 tenths
2. 2 tenths and 9 tenths
3. 4 tenths and 8 tenths
4. 3 units 9 tenths and 1 unit 6 tenths
5. 4 units 7 tenths and 6 units 7 tenths
6. $5\frac{2}{10}$ and $2\frac{2}{10}$ 8. $3\frac{6}{10}$ and $6\frac{4}{10}$
7. $4\frac{9}{10}$ and $1\frac{9}{10}$ 9. $\frac{8}{10}$, $\frac{7}{10}$ and $\frac{6}{10}$.

Write as a decimal the difference between:

10. 1.0 and 0.1   15. 10.0 and 9.8
11. 1.3 and 2.0   16. 1.1 and 0.7
12. 2.0 and 0.2   17. 3.5 and 2.6
13. 5.6 and 6.0   18. 20.8 and 19.9
14. 4.0 and 3.4   19. 17.3 and 16.5.

Write the answers only.

20. 1.3+2.6   26. 4.0−2.5
21. 4.8+2.2   27. 2.7−1.8
22. 3.7+4.3   28. 7.2−4.4
23. 7.5+2.5   29. 10.6−4.7
24. 1.9+2.4   30. 3.1−1.9
25. 8.6+3.9   31. 7.3−5.6

B Write and complete the following.

1. 893 = ☐ hundreds ☐ tens ☐ units
2. 702 = ☐ hundreds ☐ tens ☐ units
3. 25.8 = ☐ tens ☐ units ☐ tenths
4. 30.5 = ☐ tens ☐ units ☐ tenths
5. 86.6 = ☐ tens ☐ units ☐ tenths

Write the answers only.

6. 500+40+8   11. 100+4+0.2
7. 2000+800+20   12. 1000+700+0.1
8. 60+0.3   13. 300+0.5
9. 70+9+0.6   14. 4000+50+0.7
10. 700+90+0.4   15. 2000+6+0.6

Write these fractions:
   a   as tenths   b   as decimals.

16. $\frac{1}{2}$ 17. $\frac{1}{5}$ 18. $\frac{3}{5}$ 19. $\frac{4}{5}$

C Write the following as decimals.

1. 9 tens, 4 units, 3 tenths
2. 65 units, 8 tenths
3. 5 hundreds, 9 units, 7 tenths
4. 3 tens, 9 tenths   7. 22 tenths
5. 81 tenths   8. 140 tenths
6. 100 tenths   9. 237 tenths

Read the answers to your partner who will check them from the answer book.

Give the letter of the column in which the value of the 4 is:

$$\begin{array}{ccccc} v & w & x & y & z \\ 4 & 4 & 4 & 4 & . & 4 \end{array}$$

10. 4 units
11. 4 hundreds   13. 4 thousands
12. 4 tens   14. 4 tenths.

D Look at these numbers.

1. By how many times does the value of the 3 increase each time it is moved one place to the left?

3 3 3 3 . 3   to the left ←

2. By how many times does the value of the 7 decrease each time it is moved one place to the right?

7 7 7 7 . 7   to the right →

How many times bigger is:

3. 20 than 2   4. 200 than 20
5. 80 than 8   6. 800 than 80
7. 750 than 75   8. 1000 than 100
9. 1500 than 150   10. 2060 than 206?

How many times smaller is:

11. 3 than 30   12. 30 than 300
13. 5 than 50   14. 50 than 500
15. 64 than 640   16. 200 than 2000
17. 390 than 3900   18. 108 than 1080?

What is the value of each figure underlined in these numbers?

19. 7752   20. 344.8   21. 86.6
22. 105.5   23. 284.3   24. 19.4

Sets

A

A set is a collection of things which are alike in some way.

Examples
John has a set of model cars.
Mary has a set of coloured pencils.
Mother has a set of golf-clubs.
Father has a set of spanners.

There are sets in your class-room.

Examples
The set of children who wear spectacles
The set of children who are girls
The set of books in the library

1   Think of other sets of things or people and name six sets which you have at home or at school.

Each thing in a set is called a **member** of the set.

2   Write five members of the set of numbers less than 6.

Capital letters are used to name sets.

Look at the pictures above.

The pictures can be sorted into four sets.

3   Describe each of the sets and name each set with a capital letter.
The first is done for you.

Set W is a set of wild flowers.

Set S is a set of _____.

Set N is a set of _____.

Set C is a set of _____.

4   How many members are there in each set?

B

Look at the sets F and B.
The members of each set have been placed in a ring or box to show that they are a set.

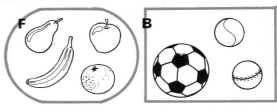

1   Find a name which describes each set.
Write and complete:
F is a set of _____

B is a set of _____.

How many members are there in

2   Set F   3   Set B?

These are the members of the Smith family.

Mr Smith, Mrs Smith, Tim Smith

The set of the Smith family can be shown in the following ways:

S =   (Mr Smith, Mrs Smith, Tim Smith)

or by placing the members of the set in brackets.

S = {Mr Smith, Mrs Smith, Tim Smith}
S = {members of the Smith family}

The brackets { } mean 'the set of'.

Notice the commas which separate the members of a set.

4   Use a capital letter and list in brackets the members of each of these sets.

N = {three girls' names}

P = {four pets}

V = {letters called vowels}

X = {five squares}

5   Give the reason why you are told how many members to write in sets N, P and X.

£s and pence counting money

A

1 Find the total of the coins in the box.

2 Name four of the coins which would be used to pay for a notebook costing 18p.

3 How much money would be left?

Find the least number of the coins which can be used to pay these sums of money. Name the coins.

4 16p	5 14p	6 21p	7 53p
8 70p	9 7p	10 69p	11 62p

Which four of the coins make:

12 37p	13 19p	14 63p	15 22p
16 15p	17 85p	18 10p	19 40p?

In the table you are shown three ways of making up 10p by using FIVES, TWOS or pennies.

5p	2p	1p
		10
	1	8
	2	6

20 Draw the table and write all the other different ways you can find.
(Altogether there are 10 different ways.)

B

Sums of money less than £1·00 can be written in two ways. e.g.

67p or £0·67   7p or £0·07
50p or £0·50

> **Remember**
> The dot or point separates the £s from the pence.

Write the following as £s, using the £ sign and a point.

1 17p	2 39p	3 10p	4 2p
5 80p	6 96p	7 5p	8 9p

Write the following as pence, using the 'p' sign only.

9 £0·74	10 £0·46	11 £0·60	12 £0·06
13 £0·04	14 £0·50	15 £0·11	16 £0·01

Write the total value of each of the following, first as pence and then as £s.

17 1 FIFTY, 3 TENS and 2 TWOS

18 7 TENS, 3 FIVES and 4 pence

19 1 TWENTY, 1 TEN and 4 TWOS

20 1 FIFTY, 1 TWENTY and 10 pence

C

David gave the shopkeeper 3 TENS to pay for a book which cost 22p. The shopkeeper gave him his change by **counting on** from the price.

The shopkeeper said:
22p and **1p** make 23p and a **TWO** make 25p and a **FIVE** make 30p.

1 How much change did David receive?

In the same way, using the least number, name the coins given in change from the following. Give the total of the change in each case.

a TEN	1 TWENTY	3 TENS	2 TWENTIES	1 FIFTY	£1
amount spent	amount spent	amount spent	amount spent	amount spent	amount spent
2 4p	5 13p	8 27p	11 21p	14 39p	17 48p
3 7p	6 16p	9 22p	12 38p	15 14p	18 63p
4 6p	7 11p	10 25p	13 22p	16 25p	19 29p

£s and pence counting money

A

1 These are the coins John has saved.
Starting with the coins of the highest value, find the total value of all the coins.

B

> **Remember**
> If the total is 100p or more, it must be written as £s.

Find the total value of the money in each of the rows below.

£1	50	20	10	5	2	1
1		2	2	3	5	2
2	1	1	1	4	2	
3	1		4	4	3	3
4	2	3	2	1	6	10	6

5 Ask your teacher for some bags of mixed coins. Practise sorting and counting them to find the total in each bag.

Look carefully at the columns below in which the sums of money are written.

6 £1, 9 TENS, 6p
7 £2 and 39p

£		
1 ·	9	6
2 ·	3	9

Copy the columns and in the same way write in the following sums of money. Make sure that each figure is in its correct place.

8 £3, 4 TENS, 2p
9 £2 and 60p
10 309p
11 £5 and 3 TENS
12 6 TENS and 4p
13 13 TENS and 5p
14 40p
15 30 TENS and 2p
16 9p
17 70 TENS

C

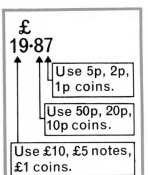

£ 19·87

Use 5p, 2p, 1p coins.

Use 50p, 20p, 10p coins.

Use £10, £5 notes, £1 coins.

Study the diagram. It shows the notes and coins to use when paying sums of money.

Name the notes and coins, using as few as possible, to pay each of these amounts.

1 £4·50   2 £6·10   3 £12·05
4 £3·30   5 £5·62   6 £11·27
7 £0·28   8 £0·83   9 £10·79

How many TENS can be given for:
10 £1·70   11 £3·50   12 £4·00
13 £2·10   14 £5·90   15 £7·20
16 £6·60   17 £8·00   18 £10·00?

Write and complete:
19 £2·68 = ☐ TENS ☐ p
20 £4·03 = ☐ TENS ☐ p
21 £9·30 = ☐ TENS ☐ p
22 £0·05 = ☐ TENS ☐ p.

Find the value of the figure 6 in each of these sums of money.
23 £0·63   24 £6·32   25 £1·06
26 £6·01   27 £5·16   28 £3·60

Symmetry shapes which balance

A Look at the drawings below.

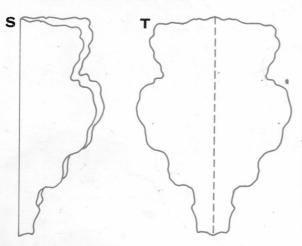

Drawing **S** shows a piece of paper folded in half along a vertical fold line and a pattern torn around the fold.

Drawing **T** shows the torn paper opened out. Notice that each half of the shape balances about the fold line.

1 In the same way, fold a piece of paper in half along a vertical fold line and tear or cut out a pattern around the fold.

2 Open the torn-out piece and mark the fold with a dotted line.

3 Do the two halves balance about the dotted line?

4 Repeat the exercise, but this time make a horizontal fold, as shown below. Make an interesting pattern and mark the fold or 'balance' line.

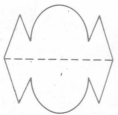

5 Fold other pieces of paper and, in the same way, draw and cut out some interesting shapes, using a vertical or horizontal fold.

6 Mark the balance line in each case.

B A line about which a shape balances is called a **line of symmetry**.

Shapes which balance are called **symmetrical shapes**.

1 On cm squared paper, copy the drawings below.

2 Cut them out and draw the dotted line in each.

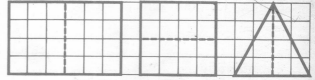

3 Fold each shape along the dotted line.

4 Is the dotted line in each a line of symmetry? How do you know?

5 On cm squared paper, draw the shapes below and then mark the vertical line of symmetry in each.

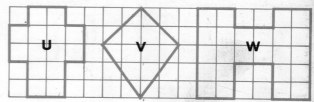

6 Now cut out the shapes and fold each along the line of symmetry you have drawn. If, in any of the shapes, the two parts do not balance when folded, draw the shape again and find the correct line of symmetry.

7 On cm squared paper, draw the shapes below and then mark the horizontal line of symmetry in each.

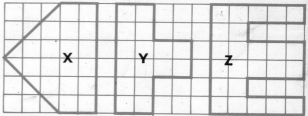

8 Cut out the shapes and then check by folding that you have drawn each balance line correctly.

Symmetry

A Some shapes have oblique lines of symmetry.

1 Copy the following shapes on cm squared paper.

2 On each, draw an oblique line of symmetry.

3 Then cut out each shape and check each line of symmetry by folding.

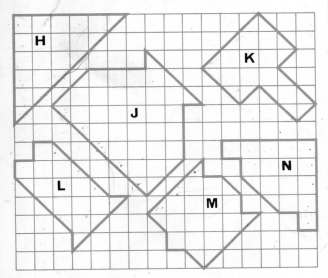

Look at the drawings below.
Each is a half-shape and a line of symmetry is shown by a dotted line.

4 Draw half-shape **O** on cm squared paper and then complete the shape.

5 In the same way, draw and complete shapes **P**, **Q**, **R**, **S** and **T**.

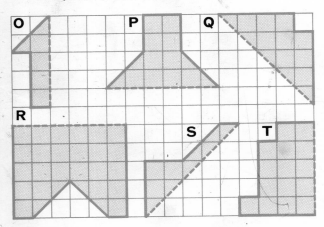

B Some shapes have more than one line of symmetry.

1 On squared paper, draw and cut out a large square.

2 By folding, find how many lines of symmetry there are in the square.

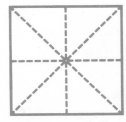

3 a Draw and cut out two other squares of different sizes.
  b By folding, find how many lines of symmetry there are in each square.

4 Get four rectangular pieces of paper.

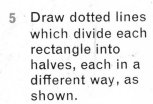

5 Draw dotted lines which divide each rectangle into halves, each in a different way, as shown.

6 Fold each rectangle along the dotted line to find which of these are lines of symmetry.

Remember that in each case, one half must fit exactly over the other half.

7 How many lines of symmetry has a rectangle?

8 Draw a rectangle in your book and show the lines of symmetry.

> Lines of symmetry can be vertical, horizontal or oblique.
>
> Some shapes have more than one line of symmetry.

Addition and subtraction facts

Place a strip
of paper
alongside test **A**
and write the
answers only.

Go on to tests
B, C and **D** in
the same way.

Time yourself for
the four tests.

Beat the clock
6 minutes for
the four tests

---

	to 10			to 10			to 18			to 18
A		**B**			**C**			**D**		
1	2+4	1	10−8		1	9+5		1	13−6	
2	8+0	2	9−3		2	7+7		2	11−9	
3	7+3	3	7−4		3	8+4		3	14−7	
4	5+5	4	9−9		4	9+2		4	15−8	
5	1+8	5	6−3		5	6+7		5	13−9	
6	2+6	6	8−2		6	8+9		6	11−5	
7	0+7	7	9−4		7	5+6		7	14−8	
8	1+6	8	7−7		8	8+3		8	12−7	
9	5+3	9	8−3		9	9+9		9	15−9	
10	10+0	10	10−5		10	6+6		10	12−6	
11	6+4	11	9−8		11	8+7		11	16−8	
12	7+1	12	6−4		12	3+9		12	13−5	
13	2+5	13	10−9		13	5+8		13	17−9	
14	4+3	14	9−7		14	4+9		14	12−3	
15	2+8	15	8−4		15	7+5		15	16−7	
16	1+9	16	5−5		16	6+9		16	11−4	
17	5+4	17	8−7		17	8+6		17	18−9	
18	2+7	18	10−4		18	9+7		18	14−5	
19	6+3	19	7−5		19	8+8		19	11−8	
20	4+4	20	10−7		20	4+7		20	12−4	

Mark the answers and correct any mistakes in full.

Make sure you know these facts. Practise again and again
until you can write the answers correctly and beat the clock.

Draw this table.

Keep a record of the results
whenever you work these tests.

+ −	date				
time in min					
number correct					

E **Bridging the tens** Write the answers only.

1	22+9	7	52−9	13	86+8	19	84−6	25	9+39
2	34+8	8	75−7	14	55+7	20	53−7	26	8+75
3	47+9	9	33−4	15	39+6	21	67−8	27	6+87
4	73+8	10	66−9	16	69+8	22	42−5	28	8+49
5	55+9	11	41−6	17	77+4	23	25−6	29	4+69
6	67+6	12	91−7	18	47+8	24	83−8	30	8+28

F Find the value of each letter.

$9 + a = 6 + 4$ $\quad$ $11 − 2 = 18 − c$ $\quad$ $4 + 5 = 10 − e$ $\quad$ $58 − 9 = 40 + g$

$6 + 9 = b + 7$ $\quad$ $13 − d = 11 − 4$ $\quad$ $f − 3 = 5 + 2$ $\quad$ $h + 20 = 34 + 7$

Graphs

A

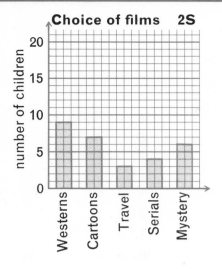

Choice of films   2S

The children in Class 2S were asked which kind of film they liked best.

The block graph shows the result.

1 From how many kinds of films could they choose?

2 Which kind of film was the most popular?

3 Write the films in order, putting the most popular one first.

4 Find the total number of children who took part.

At the bottom of the graph is a **horizontal line**.

5 What is shown on this line?

At the side of the graph is a **vertical line**.

6 What is shown on this line?

7 What does one division on this line stand for?

These two lines have special names. One is called the **horizontal axis** and the other the **vertical axis**.

B

Anthony asked the children in classes 2M and 2A which kind of film they liked best.

First, he made this record sheet.

Then the choice of each child was shown by a mark (*I*) placed against the chosen kind of film. Notice that *IIII* stands for 5.

films	choices	totals
Westerns	IIII IIII IIII IIII	
Cartoons	IIII IIII IIII II	
Travel	IIII II	
Serials	IIII IIII	
Mystery	IIII	

1 Find the total number of children who chose each kind of film.

2 Draw a block graph of the results.

3 Find the total number of children who took part.

4 Write their choices in order, putting the most popular first.

5 Compare the order with that in **A3**. What differences are there?

C

Anthony made the record sheet below and on it he recorded the choices of classes 2S, 2M and 2A together.

films	choices	totals
Westerns	IIII IIII IIII IIII IIII IIII	
Cartoons	IIII IIII IIII IIII IIII	
Travel	IIII IIII	
Serials	IIII IIII III	
Mystery	IIII IIII I	

1 Find the total number of children who chose each kind of film.

2 Draw a block graph of the results.

3 Find the total number of children who took part.

4 Write their choices in order, putting the most popular first.

5 In the same way, make a record by asking each of the children in your class to make a choice.

6 Draw a graph of the results.

7 Write these choices in order, putting the most popular first.

8 Compare the first three choices with the first three in **A3** and **B4**.

Graphs

A Clare made a record sheet to find which was the favourite sweet of 100 children who stayed at school for dinner.

The graph shows the results.

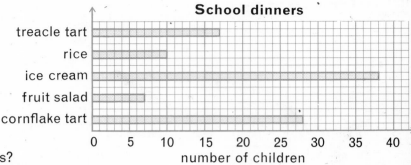

1 On which axis are the sweets shown?

2 What does one division stand for on the horizontal axis?

3 How many children liked each kind of sweet? Write and complete the answers like this:
☐ out of 100 children chose treacle tart.
☐ out of 100 children chose rice, and so on.

4 Write the sweets in order, putting the most popular first.

B Vowels = {a, e, i, o, u}

Nearly every word contains one or more vowels.

1 Write your name in full and the name of your school.

2 Count how many times each vowel is used.

Susan made a count of the vowels from two sentences in her reading book.

She then made this graph of the result.

The use of vowels

(graph: vowels a, e, i, o, u on vertical axis; number of times used 0, 5, 10, 15, 20, 25 on horizontal axis)

3 How many times was each vowel used?

4 Which vowel was used most frequently?

5 Write the vowels in order, putting the one used most times first.

From the graph find:

6 which vowel was used five times more than the vowel u

7 the two vowels used the same number of times.

C Peter made this record of vowels used in a paragraph of his book.

vowels	times used	totals
a	ЖЖ ЖЖ ЖЖ l	
e	ЖЖ ЖЖ ЖЖ ЖЖ ЖЖ lll	
i	ЖЖ ЖЖ	
o	ЖЖ ЖЖ ЖЖ ЖЖ ll	
u	ЖЖ ЖЖ llll	

1 Draw a graph of the count, showing the vowels on the vertical axis and the numbers on the horizontal axis.

2 From the graph, answer the questions **B4** and **B5**.

3 Make a record of the vowels in the following.
Jean and Peter went for a day to London where they visited the Houses of Parliament, Westminster Abbey and the Tower. They also wished to go to the Zoo but unfortunately it began to rain.

4 Draw a graph of the count, showing the vowels on the horizontal axis and the numbers on the vertical axis.

5 Select a paragraph from a story-book. Make a count of the vowels and draw a graph. Compare your results with those in **C4**.

Shapes   the square and the rhombus

The square and the rhombus are members of the set of quadrilaterals.
Any shape which has four straight sides is called a quadrilateral.

A

1 Using a ruler and a set square, draw on a sheet of paper a square of 8 cm side. Cut it out.

2 By measuring in mm, find if the opposite sides are parallel.

3 Draw a diagonal and cut along it. You have made two triangles.

4 Is the diagonal a line of symmetry?

5 Fit one triangle on to the other. Are they the same shape and size?

6 What fraction of the square is each triangle?

B

1 Draw and cut out another 8 cm square. Draw the two diagonals.

2 Are they equal in length?

3 Mark the point at which the diagonals **bisect** each other. ('bisect' means cut into two equal parts)

Find, by measuring in mm, that:

4 the diagonals bisect each other

5 the point is the centre of the square.

6 Are the four angles at the centre right angles?

7 Both diagonals are lines of symmetry. Draw the other two lines of symmetry.

8 Write and complete the following.

> A square has _____ equal sides.
> The opposite sides are _____.
> Its four angles are _____ angles.
> The diagonals are of _____ length.
> The diagonals _____ each other.
> The angles at the centre are _____ angles.
> A square has ☐ lines of symmetry.

C

1 Get four plastic or cardboard strips of the same length and fasten them together to make a square.

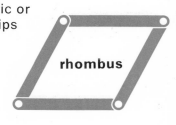

rhombus

2 Hold the bottom strip firmly and push the top strip sideways to make a different shape.

3 This new shape is called a **rhombus.** Draw it.

4 Make other rhombuses by pushing the other strips sideways. Draw them.

D

1 On gummed paper, draw and cut out a large rectangle.

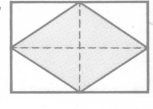

2 Fold it into four equal parts as shown by the dotted lines in the diagram.

3 Join the ends of the fold lines.

4 You have drawn a rhombus. Cut it out and stick it on a sheet of paper.

5 Four triangles were left when the rhombus was cut out. Arrange them to make another rhombus and stick it on a sheet of paper.

6 Draw another large rectangle and from it cut out another rhombus.

7 By folding, find the number of lines of symmetry in a rhombus.

What can you discover about:

8 the length of the diagonals

9 the angles at the centre of the rhombus?

10 Find, by measuring, if the diagonals bisect each other.

Shapes the rectangle and the parallelogram

The rectangle and the parallelogram are members of the set of quadrilaterals.

A

Using a ruler and a set square, draw on a sheet of paper a rectangle 9 cm long and 5 cm wide. Cut it out.

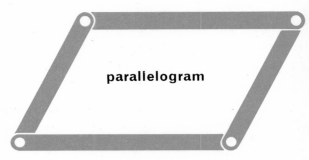

1 By measuring in mm, find if the opposite sides are parallel.

2 Draw a diagonal.

3 How many triangles have you made?

4 Fold the rectangle along the diagonal.

5 Do the triangles fit exactly?

6 Is the diagonal a line of symmetry?

7 Cut along the diagonal. Place one triangle on the other. How must you place them so that they fit exactly?

8 What fraction of the rectangle is each triangle?

Draw and cut out another rectangle 9 cm by 5 cm.

9 Draw the two diagonals.

10 Measure each diagonal in mm.

11 What do you discover?

12 Do the diagonals bisect each other?

Four angles are formed where the diagonals bisect each other.

13 Use a set square to find how many of the angles are:
a right angles
b less than a right angle
c greater than a right angle.

14 By folding, find the number of lines of symmetry in a rectangle.

15 Cut along the diagonals and so make four triangles. By fitting these triangles one on top of another, what can you find about their size and shape?

B

1 Get four plastic or cardboard strips and fasten them together to make a rectangle.

2 Hold the bottom strip firmly and push the top strip sideways to make a different shape.

3 This new shape is called a **parallelogram**. Draw it.

parallelogram

4 Make other parallelograms by pushing the other strips sideways. Draw them.

C

1 On gummed paper, draw and cut out a large rectangle.

2 Draw a diagonal and cut along it.

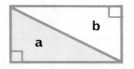 

3 You now have two triangles. Fit them together to make a parallelogram, as shown, and stick it on a sheet of paper.

4 In the same way, make other parallelograms from rectangles of different sizes.

What can you discover about:
5 the sides of a parallelogram
6 the diagonals   7 the angles?

8 Draw and cut out a parallelogram. Find, by folding, how many lines of symmetry it has.

Addition   number and money

First work group **A**. Mark the answers and correct any mistakes.
Then work groups **B** to **G** in the same way.
Write the answers only.

First add upwards, then check by adding downwards.

A

1	2	3	4	5
141	62	219	108	107
16	205	145	38	127
+223	+ 32	+206	+114	+356

B

1	2	3	4	5
212	244	225	238	105
63	326	537	304	49
+318	+104	+123	+355	+544

C

1	2	3	4	5
32	193	661	488	164
260	173	63	350	351
+257	+172	+135	+170	+364

D

1	2	3	4	5
167	598	306	149	97
107	92	387	76	94
+462	+241	+ 38	+103	+187

6	7	8	9	10
187	297	788	3369	1459
750	878	689	4169	478
+137	+237	+168	+2179	+1397

Write the answers as £s.

E

1	2	3	4	5
£	£	£	£	£
0·27	0·05	0·15	0·14	0·09
0·48	0·63	0·08	0·26	0·75
+0·17	+0·24	+0·39	+0·26	+0·15

F

1	2	3	4	5
£	£	£	£	£
0·74	0·69	0·89	0·68	0·45
0·29	0·29	0·37	0·48	0·59
+0·18	+0·14	+0·19	+0·48	+0·19

G

1	2	3	4	5
£	£	£	£	£
4·86	22·45	15·45	32·89	18·59
0·53	32·93	1·42	12·30	17·24
+1·42	+12·15	+10·74	+43·72	+ 3·94

H Write the following in vertical columns and find each total in £s.

1 £1·37, £3·24, £0·39   2 28p, 49p, 33p   3 £0·74, £3·46, £4·22

4 94p, 24p, £5·42   5 17p, 63p, 72p   6 £11·85, 79p, £1·30

Subtraction   number and money

First work group **A**. Mark the answers and correct any mistakes.
Then work groups **B** to **F** in the same way.
Write the answers only.

Check each answer by adding it to the line above.

A
| 1 | 378
−358 | 2 | 597
− 93 | 3 | 466
−420 | 4 | 955
− 45 | 5 | 972
−402 |

B
| 1 | 480
−253 | 2 | 510
−304 | 3 | 506
−254 | 4 | 408
−193 | 5 | 706
−265 |
| 6 | 900
−536 | 7 | 200
−111 | 8 | 800
−107 | 9 | 300
− 89 | 10 | 400
−330 |

C
1	971 −749	2	896 −467	3	768 −139	4	982 −373	5	785 −668
6	638 −262	7	379 −188	8	925 −870	9	548 −450	10	615 −531
11	3245 − 577	12	5597 −2599	13	6343 −1365	14	2181 − 494	15	8426 − 578

Write the answers as £s.

D
| 1 | £
4·05
−3·03 | 2 | £
13·70
− 9·70 | 3 | £
1·34
−0·99 | 4 | £
0·82
−0·56 | 5 | £
3·77
−2·04 |

E
| 1 | £
5·00
−2·44 | 2 | £
3·10
−1·20 | 3 | £
6·07
−1·09 | 4 | £
12·50
− 1·78 | 5 | £
10·00
− 1·93 |

F
| 1 | £
15·15
− 9·56 | 2 | £
28·23
− 9·37 | 3 | £
16·21
− 7·87 | 4 | £
14·03
− 5·58 | 5 | £
33·96
−25·99 |

G   Write the following in vertical columns and find each answer in £s.

1 £5·50−77p   2 £5·33−48p   3 £6·08−£1·80   4 £1·50−64p

5 £10·00−£3·52   6 £20·75−£16·80   7 £1·31−£0·38   8 £20·00−£2·20

Number and money   addition and subtraction

A

Increase:

1 972 by 89
2 £3·65 by 38p.

Find the difference between:

3 756 and 2600
4 47p and £1·20.

What must be added to:

5 276 to make 1000
6 56p to make £2·00?

Find the total of:

7 74p, 35p, 29p and 7p

8 £1·09, 53p, £2·40 and 12p.

Decrease:

9 £5·32 by 87p
10 £105 by £87.

Find the sum of:

11 97p, £1·35, 33p and 9p

12 120, 180, 1240 and 60.

Subtract:

13 3 TENS from 83p

14 £1·29 from 4 FIFTIES.

15 How much greater is the total of £1·39 and £3·87 than £5·00?

16 How much greater is the total of £5·37 and £4·63 than the sum of £3·86 and £4·75?

B

The chart shows the attendance for one week at Vale Junior School.

	Mon.	Tues.	Wed.	Thurs.	Fri.
a.m.	293	289	290	301	276
p.m.	287	271	284	298	269

Find the total number of children present:

1 in the mornings
2 in the afternoons.

3 What was the total attendance for the whole week?

4 There are 303 children at Vale Junior School. Find the highest possible attendance for the whole week.

Look at the chart below which shows the attendance at the school's May Fair (the number of girls is not shown)

May Fair - Attendance			
boys	girls	adults	total
139		364	660

5 How many children went to the Fair?
6 How many girls attended?
7 How many more adults than children were there?
8 How many more girls than boys attended?

C

The chart shows the savings of four children.

	£s	50p	20p	10p	5p
Jane	5	2	2	8	4
Michael	4	4	5	9	3
John	5		1	13	7
Wendy	3	5	3	4	9

1 Write the name of each child and the total amount each has saved.

2 How much less than £8 has Jane saved?

3 How much more has Wendy saved than John?

4 Find the total amount saved by the four children.

Classes 1 to 5 each decided to collect £10 for the N.S.P.C.C. After two weeks they had saved these amounts.

classes	1	2	3	4	5
amount saved	£7·87	£8·25	£6·28	£9·15	£7·32

5 How much short of the target of £10 was each class?

6 How much had they saved altogether?

7 How much more had class 4 saved than class 5?

Number and money addition and subtraction

A The chart shows the number of people who attended the swimming-pool for one week.

Kenton Swimming-pool			
	boys	girls	adults
Mon.	39	28	34
Tues.	70	56	80
Wed.	24	42	17
Thurs.	68	37	54
Sat.	103	91	110
Sun.	57	35	169

1 On which day was the pool closed?

Find the total number of:
2 boys   3 girls   4 adults
who attended during the week.

How many more adults attended the pool than:
5 boys   6 girls?

On which day was there:
7 the highest attendance
8 the lowest attendance?

9 Find the value of each letter.
37 + **a** = 73   48 + 24 = **b**
c − 15 = 41   68 − **d** = 29
42 + **e** = 71   **f** − 37 = 82

10 Add 29 to each of these numbers.
18   25   37   56
64   83   79   92

11 Subtract 18 from each of these numbers.
41   64   83   72
57   90   105   206

12 Look at the numbers in the box.

120	235	161
258	198	305

From the sum of the odd numbers, subtract the sum of the even numbers.

B Find the total of each of these supermarket bills. Write the answers only.

1
£0·13
£0·26
£0·35
£0·52

2
£1·10
£0·22
£0·45
£0·86

3
£0·07
£0·69
£0·94
£0·78

4 For each bill, find the change from a £5 note.

It is important to check the total cost of items and the change given.

Practise adding and finding the change from the given amounts, as in the examples below.

Find the change from a FIFTY after spending:
5 14p + 5p + 9p + 6p
6 6p + 15p + 7p + 9p
7 7p + 13p + 16p + 7p
8 9p + 8p + 3p + 5p + 15p.

> To add items costing more than 10p, first add the TENS and then the pence. e.g.
> **39**p + **46**p
> say
> **39**p + **40**p make 79p and **6**p makes **85**p

Write the answers only.
9 36p + 15p   14 19p + 78p
10 29p + 12p   15 26p + 18p
11 54p + 26p   16 55p + 28p
12 37p + 13p   17 43p + 39p
13 47p + 25p   18 68p + 17p

Find the change from £1 after spending:
19 27p + 18p + 4p   22 31p + 18p + 26p
20 24p + 27p + 7p   23 46p + 28p + 8p
21 35p + 29p + 5p   24 18p + 9p + 7p.
25 Practise with your partner making up your own shopping bills and finding the change.

Time the clock

A

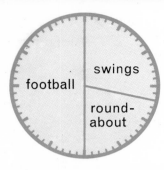

This clock face shows how Peter spent one hour in the park.

1 How many minutes are shown on the clock face?
Write and complete: 1 hour (h) = ☐ minutes (min).

2 a How many minutes were spent playing football?
  b What fraction of an hour was this?

3 How many minutes were spent on:
  a the swings   b the roundabout?

4 How much less than a quarter of an hour was spent on the roundabout?

B

Time on a clock can be stated in figures or in words.

> **a.m.** shows morning times
> **p.m.** shows afternoon or evening times

e.g. **8.50 a.m.** or ten minutes to nine in the morning

7.15 p.m. or quarter past seven in the evening

Write these times in words.

1 6.25 a.m.   2 11.56 p.m.   3 9.40 a.m.

Write these times in figures.

4 half past twelve in the afternoon
5 quarter of an hour before midnight
6 five and twenty minutes to ten in the evening
7 thirteen minutes before noon
8 twenty-seven minutes past eight in the morning

C

1 Write the times shown on these clocks in figures and then in words.

afternoon   morning   evening   morning

a   b   c   d

What is the correct time if:

2 clock **a** is 5 min slow
3 clock **b** is 5 min fast

4 clock **c** is a quarter of an hour slow
5 clock **d** is 20 min fast?

D

How many minutes are there between:

1 10 o'clock and quarter to eleven
2 quarter to four and ten past four
3 half past twelve and quarter past one
4 3.47 p.m. and 4.00 p.m.
5 2.50 p.m. and 3.23 p.m.
6 8.45 a.m. and 9.12 a.m.?

How many h and min are there from:

7 7.30 a.m. to 9.15 a.m.
8 8.20 p.m. to 10.10 p.m.
9 10.25 a.m. to noon
10 8.45 p.m. to midnight
11 2.50 p.m. to 6.00 p.m.
12 3.30 p.m. to 5.05 p.m.?

E

Write in figures the time when you:

1 went to bed last night
2 got up this morning   3 set off for school.

Find in hours and minutes how long you spent:

4 in bed   5 in getting ready for school.

Time minutes and seconds

A When it is necessary to measure short periods of time very carefully, **seconds (s)** are used.

This is a watch face which has a coloured second hand.

1 How many seconds have passed when the second hand makes one complete turn?

How many seconds are there in:

2 1 min   3 $\frac{1}{2}$ min   4 $\frac{1}{4}$ min?

5 Look at a watch with a second hand. Count slowly in seconds 1, 2, 3, 4, 5 up to 60.

6 Try this again and again until you can count second by second to a minute. Ask your partner to test you.

B Work with a partner, taking turns with a watch which has a second hand.

1 Find how many words you can write neatly in one minute, starting from the top of this page.

2 Turn to page 12 and find how many of the answers to the examples you can write in 1 minute.

3 Take turns with your partner to estimate the time in seconds to complete each of the activities listed in the chart below.

Draw the chart to make a record of your estimates.

Then find the actual time for each.

activity	time in seconds		
	estimate	actual	error
writing your address			
walking across the room			
saying the 5 times table			

4 Write other activities in your chart which you think will take one minute or less.

5 Then estimate and time them.

C A stop-watch is used for making accurate measurements of time in s or min and s.

It can be used for timing races on Sports Day.

1 Get a stop-watch.

2 Find out how to stop and start it and how to read the minutes and seconds shown on the dial.

3 How many minutes and seconds are shown on the dial in the picture?

4 Still working with a partner, estimate the time taken to complete each of the activities listed in the table below.

Then, find the actual time for each, by using a stop-watch.

Keep a record of your work.

activities	estimate		actual	
	min	s	min	s
read a page of your book				
walk round the playground				

5 Think of other activities which will take more than one minute.
Then estimate and time them.

6 Find the time taken to count 50 sheets of paper. At this rate, how long will it take to count:

7 100 sheets   8 200 sheets?

9 In the playground, measure and mark a distance of 50 metres.

10 Find the number of seconds it takes to walk 50 metres.

At this rate, find how many min and s it will take you to walk:

11 100 m   12 1000 m or 1 km.

If you telephone Timeline for the speaking clock, you will hear: "At the third stroke the time will be . . .", and it will be given in hours, minutes and seconds. Try it.

Measuring temperature

A You will need a Celsius thermometer like the one shown.

There may be one in your class-room which is used for measuring the hotness or coldness (the **temperature**) of the air.

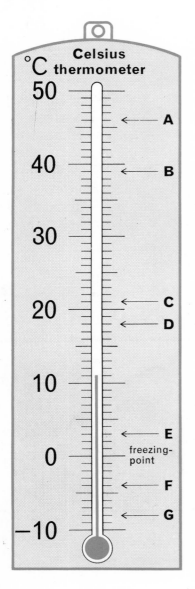

1 Examine the thermometer and you will find that it is a sealed glass tube which is partly filled with a liquid, usually alcohol or mercury.

2 Breathe several times on to the bulb at the bottom of the tube. Watch the level of the liquid. What happens?

3 When you stop breathing warm air on to the bulb, what happens to the level of the liquid?

4 What have you discovered about the temperature of the air you breathe out and that of the air in the class-room?

5 Place the thermometer in a bowl of cold water. Watch the level of the liquid in the tube. Which is the warmer, the water or the air?

6 The level of the liquid in the tube rises or falls with the changes of temperature. Find the reason for this.

B Temperatures are measured on the scale marked alongside the tube.

The unit of measurement is called a **degree Celsius** shown by **°C**.

Look at the scale on the picture of the thermometer.

1 How many degrees does one small division represent?

2 Write the temperature at which water freezes (the **freezing-point**). Notice that a minus sign (−) shows temperatures below freezing-point.

3 Write the highest and the lowest temperatures which can be measured on this thermometer.

4 Read the temperature shown by the level of the liquid.

What would be the reading if the temperature were:

5 12°C warmer   6 12°C colder?

7 Write the temperatures at the points marked **A, B, C, D, E, F** and **G**.

Measure the temperature of the air:

8 inside the class-room   9 in the playground.

10 Find the difference between the two temperatures.

Making sure

A
Write the answers only.

1	2	3
1860	2045	4196
935	487	756
+ 288	+3499	+2048

Write the following in vertical columns and then find the total of each.

4 94+2067+328

5 640+900+4778

6 £0·57+£20·15+£6·30

7 £1·38+£0·79+£2·47

8 £12·00+£18·37+£6·50

Write the answers only.

9	10	11
4870	2607	2333
−1984	−1796	−1874

12 316−56   13 254−85   14 426−99

15 590−145   16 185−97   17 930−710

B
Copy the chart below and write the coins (using as few as possible) to pay for each of the given amounts.

The first is done for you.

	amount	50p	20p	10p	5p	2p
1	9p				1	2
2	34p					
3	70p					
4	17p					
5	65p					
6	24p					

How many TENS have the same value as:

7 £2·30   8 £4·80   9 £5·10   10 £6·40?

Find the total of each of the following.

11 3 TENS, 3 FIVES and 2 TWOS

12 8 TWOS, 5 FIVES and 9 pennies

Write the answers only.

13 50p−27p   14 50p−11p   15 50p−33p

16 £1−18p   17 £1−34p   18 £1−49p

19 (20p+10p)−22p   20 (20p+20p)−26p

C
This is part of a TV programme.

> 5.05 ___ News
> 5.15 ___ Test yourself
> 5.45 ___ Cartoons
> 6.10 ___ Space travel
> 7.05 ___ The Brown Family

How long is each of these programmes?

1 News   2 Test yourself

3 Cartoons   4 Space travel

5 There are two cartoons in the Cartoons programme. One lasts 5 minutes longer than the other.
How many minutes does each last?

How many days are there in:

6 April   7 June   8 Aug.   9 Oct.?

10 How many days are there in a leap year?

How many days are there in these months of the year?

11 the 1st   12 the 3rd

13 the 5th   14 the 7th

15 the 9th   16 the 11th

D
A boy took the temperature at midday on ten consecutive days. He made this graph.

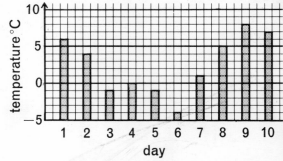

On which day was the temperature:

1 the highest   2 the lowest?

3 On which days was the temperature at freezing-point or below?

4 Find the difference between the highest and the lowest temperatures.

5 Write the temperature at midday on each of the ten days.

Multiplication and division facts

Place a strip of paper alongside test **A** and write the answers only.

Then go on to tests **B, C, D** and **E**. Mark the answers and correct any mistakes.

A		**B**		**C**		**D**		**E**	
1	7×3	1	$24 \div 4$	1	5×4	1	$36 \div 4$	1	$16 \div 4$
2	5×8	2	$12 \div 6$	2	0×7	2	$9 \div 9$	2	3×7
3	6×5	3	$16 \div 2$	3	3×6	3	$18 \div 2$	3	$81 \div 9$
4	4×7	4	$40 \div 5$	4	2×5	4	$54 \div 9$	4	2×8
5	9×3	5	$18 \div 9$	5	7×7	5	$45 \div 5$	5	$36 \div 6$
6	8×7	6	$49 \div 7$	6	8×3	6	$72 \div 9$	6	3×9
7	3×8	7	$54 \div 6$	7	9×8	7	$28 \div 7$	7	$18 \div 6$
8	4×4	8	$21 \div 7$	8	6×6	8	$32 \div 4$	8	7×4
9	9×5	9	$16 \div 8$	9	7×8	9	$48 \div 6$	9	$45 \div 9$
10	5×7	10	$18 \div 3$	10	6×9	10	$24 \div 8$	10	8×5
11	0×9	11	$63 \div 9$	11	3×4	11	$35 \div 5$	11	$20 \div 5$
12	6×8	12	$72 \div 8$	12	8×9	12	$30 \div 6$	12	9×7
13	9×9	13	$25 \div 5$	13	2×7	13	$48 \div 8$	13	$42 \div 7$
14	6×4	14	$36 \div 9$	14	5×5	14	$21 \div 3$	14	4×6
15	9×6	15	$40 \div 8$	15	9×4	15	$27 \div 9$	15	$14 \div 7$
16	3×5	16	$24 \div 6$	16	2×9	16	$56 \div 7$	16	8×8
17	7×6	17	$35 \div 7$	17	7×5	17	$64 \div 8$	17	$32 \div 8$
18	5×9	18	$24 \div 3$	18	8×6	18	$42 \div 6$	18	7×9
19	6×2	19	$63 \div 7$	19	4×8	19	$0 \div 8$	19	$56 \div 8$
20	8×4	20	$28 \div 4$	20	6×7	20	$27 \div 3$	20	4×9

Make sure you know the multiplication and division tables.

Practise again and again until you can write the answers correctly and quickly.
Try to beat the target of 10 min.

Draw this table in your book.
Keep a record of the results
whenever you work these tests.

x ÷ date				
time in min				
number correct				

F Find the value of each letter.

1		2	
$15 \div 3 = $ **a**		$32 \div $ **i** $ = 8$	
b $\times 5 = 20$		$6 \times 4 = $ **j**	
$49 \div $ **c** $ = 7$		$48 \div $ **k** $ = 8$	
$9 \times 8 = $ **d**		$5 \times 6 = $ **l**	
e $\div 9 = 4$		**m** $\div 8 = 1$	
$8 \times $ **f** $ = 64$		$7 \times $ **n** $ = 42$	
$63 \div 9 = $ **g**		$28 \div 4 = $ **o**	
h $\times 9 = 54$		**p** $\times 9 = 18$	

G A **factor** is a number which will divide exactly into another number without a remainder.
e.g. Set of factors of $12 = \{1, 2, 3, 4, 6, 12\}$

In the same way, copy and complete each set of factors below.

1 Set of factors of $16 = \{1, \square, \square, \square, 16\}$
2 Set of factors of $18 = \{1, 2, \square, \square, \square, 18\}$
3 Set of factors of $20 = \{1, \square, \square, \square, \square, 20\}$
4 Set of factors of $24 = \{1, \square, \square, \square, \square, \square, \square, 24\}$

Number multiplication and division

A

Write the answers only.

1	$(8 \times 8) + 7$	7	$6(3) + 2$	13	$76 - (8 \times 9)$	19	$9 - 4(2)$
2	$(4 \times 7) + 5$	8	$7(7) + 4$	14	$25 - (3 \times 7)$	20	$13 - 1(9)$
3	$(9 \times 2) + 1$	9	$4(5) + 4$	15	$23 - (3 \times 6)$	21	$29 - 9(3)$
4	$(7 \times 9) + 8$	10	$4(9) + 7$	16	$22 - (5 \times 4)$	22	$33 - 8(4)$
5	$(0 \times 8) + 6$	11	$8(6) + 5$	17	$69 - (9 \times 7)$	23	$47 - 7(6)$
6	$(6 \times 6) + 5$	12	$7(5) + 4$	18	$28 - (5 \times 5)$	24	$41 - 5(7)$

B

Write each missing number.

1	$6(8) + \square = 53$	4	$7(3) + \square = 25$	7	$(5 \times 9) - 7 = \square$	10	$(7 \times 4) - 3 = \square$
2	$9(8) + \square = 75$	5	$8(5) + \square = 44$	8	$(4 \times 6) - 5 = \square$	11	$(2 \times 6) - 5 = \square$
3	$6(4) + \square = 27$	6	$6(9) + \square = 60$	9	$(9 \times 5) - 4 = \square$	12	$(9 \times 9) - 8 = \square$

C

There are remainders in the answers to the following. e.g. $23 \div 6 = 3$ rem. 5
Write the answers only.

		a	b	c	d	e	f
1	Divide by 2	9	11	15	19	13	17
2	Divide by 3	20	14	22	28	17	11
3	Divide by 4	30	17	38	23	19	29
4	Divide by 5	29	34	43	47	24	18
5	Divide by 6	15	35	41	50	58	20
6	Divide by 7	19	31	46	51	62	11
7	Divide by 8	15	20	63	45	19	71
8	Divide by 9	20	42	52	32	67	80

D

1 Find the value of each letter.

$n \div 2 = 9$ rem. 1	$u \div 8 = 6$ rem. 4
$p \div 4 = 7$ rem. 3	$v \div 6 = 4$ rem. 5
$q \div 5 = 6$ rem. 2	$w \div 5 = 3$ rem. 4
$r \div 9 = 2$ rem. 7	$x \div 7 = 8$ rem. 5
$s \div 7 = 4$ rem. 6	$y \div 9 = 7$ rem. 7
$t \div 3 = 8$ rem. 2	$z \div 4 = 3$ rem. 3

Find by the shortest method:

2 $(8 + 8 + 8 + 8 + 8) + (3 + 3 + 3 + 3)$
3 $(9 + 9 + 9 + 9 + 9 + 9) + (5 + 5 + 5)$
4 $(7 + 7 + 7 + 7) + (6 + 6 + 6 + 6 + 6)$
5 $(2p + 2p + 2p + 2p) + (5p + 5p + 5p + 5p)$
6 $50p - (8p + 8p + 8p + 8p + 8p + 8p)$
7 4 TENS $- (7p + 7p + 7p + 7p + 7p)$.

E

Write each missing number.

1 $8 \times \square = 6 \times 4$	4 $\square \times 9 = 6 \times 6$
2 $\square \times 6 = 4 \times 3$	5 $5 \times \square = 10 \times 4$
3 $3 \times \square = 2 \times 9$	6 $\square \times 2 = 6 \times 3$

Find a quick way of working the following.
Write the answers only.

7 $(2 \times 3) + (3 \times 3)$ 9 $(6 \times 6) - (3 \times 6)$
8 $(5 \times 8) + (4 \times 8)$ 10 $(4 \times 5) - (3 \times 5)$

Measuring length estimating and measuring

A

1 Get a metre ruler, marked in centimetres.

How many centimetres (cm) are there in

2 1 metre   3 $\frac{1}{2}$ metre?

Write and complete, using the sign
> or < in place of ●.

4 75 cm ● $\frac{1}{2}$ m   5 56 cm ● $\frac{1}{2}$ m

6 49 cm ● $\frac{1}{2}$ m   7 35 cm ● $\frac{1}{2}$ m

Measuring to the nearest metre

When measuring lengths with a metre ruler, there is often a short length at the end which is less than one metre.

> If the short length is a **half metre or more**, count to the next metre.
> If it is **less than a half metre**, forget it.

Write these lengths to the nearest m.

8 3 m 60 cm   9 8 m 18 cm   10 7 m 53 cm

11 6 m 15 cm   12 4 m 50 cm   13 5 m 49 cm

B

1 Choose six distances in and around the class-room which are suitable to estimate and measure in metres.
e.g. lengths of rooms, corridors, etc.

2 Estimate each to the nearest metre.

3 Measure each distance in m and cm.

4 Write each measurement to the nearest metre.

5 Compare it with your estimate.

C

1 Work with a partner and choose three longer distances suitable for measuring with a 20-metre tape.
e.g. the school hall, playground, etc.

2 First mark a length of 5 m and measure this distance in paces.

3 By pacing, estimate to the nearest metre each of the three chosen distances.

4 Now measure each distance to the nearest metre, using the tape.

5 Compare each estimate and measurement.

D

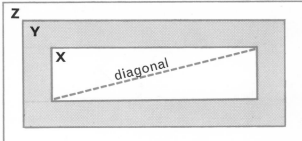

Use a ruler marked in cm and $\frac{1}{2}$ cm to measure:

1 the length

2 the width of each rectangle **X**, **Y**, **Z**.

The measurement all round a shape is called its **perimeter**.

3 Find the perimeter of each rectangle.

E

Measuring to the nearest cm

> **Remember**
> If the short length at the end is a **half cm or more**, count to the next cm.
> If it is **less than a half cm**, forget it.

A line joining the opposite corners of a rectangle is called a diagonal.

1 Measure to the nearest cm the diagonals of each of the rectangles **X**, **Y** and **Z**.

F

1 Mark the length of the span of your hand and then measure it to the nearest cm.

Using your span as a measure, find in cm:

2 the approximate length and width of your desk

3 the approximate width of the door

4 the approximate height of the door

5 the approximate height of the teacher's table.

6 Now measure each to the nearest cm.

Measuring length centimetres and millimetres

A Measuring to the nearest centimetre gives an approximate length only.

To get more accurate measurements, the **centimetre** is divided into 10 equal parts each of which is called a **millimetre   mm**.

$$1 \text{ cm} = 10 \text{ mm} \qquad 1 \text{ mm} = \tfrac{1}{10} \text{ cm} \qquad 1 \text{ mm} = 0.1 \text{ cm}$$

The drawing shows a piece of a ruler marked in centimetres and millimetres.

Notice that a millimetre is a very small unit.

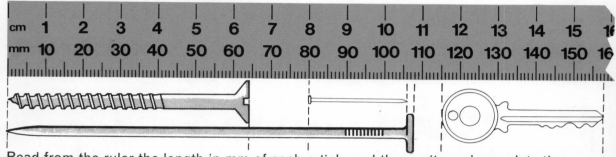

Read from the ruler the length in mm of each article and then write and complete the following.

1   The screw measures   ☐mm   or   ☐cm☐mm.
2   The nail measures   ☐mm   or   ☐cm☐mm.
3   The pin measures   ☐mm   or   ☐cm☐mm.
4   The key measures   ☐mm   or   ☐cm☐mm.

5   Get a school ruler which is marked in centimetres and millimetres.
What is the greatest length shown on it   a   in cm   b   in mm?

How many mm are there in:
6   3 cm   7   9 cm   8   10 cm   9   16 cm   10   28 cm   11   44 cm   12   50 cm?

How many cm are there in:
13   50 mm   14   70 mm   15   100 mm   16   140 mm   17   360 mm   18   580 mm   19   490 mm?

B The drawing shows a piece of a ruler.
Look at the lines below the ruler.

1   Write in mm the length of each line
R, S, T and **U**.
Line **R** is 15 mm long.
15 mm = 1 cm 5 mm = 1.5 cm

2   Write the length of
lines **S, T** and **U**:
a   in cm and mm   b   in cm.

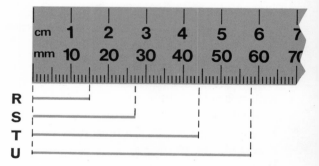

Write first as cm and mm and then as cm:
3   18 mm   4   77 mm   5   95 mm   6   109 mm   7   166 mm   8   280 mm   9   304 mm.

How many mm are there in:
10   3.7 cm   11   9.4 cm   12   10 cm   13   20.4 cm   14   37.9 cm   15   48 cm   16   70.5 cm?

Measuring length   mm   cm   m

A

1 Measure the lines **U**, **V**, **W**, **X**, **Y** and **Z** and write each length:
  a in mm   b in cm.
  Mark the answers and correct any mistakes.

  Find the total length in mm of lines:
2 **W** and **Y**   3 **V**, **X** and **Z**.
4 What is the difference in mm between the longest and the shortest lines?

  Find the total length of all the lines. Write the measurement:
5 in mm   6 in cm.
  Check the answers.

7 How many mm less than 1 metre is the total length of the lines?

8 To find the **average length** of the lines, divide the total length by the number of lines. What is the average length? Check your answer.

  By how many mm is:
9 the shortest line less than the average
10 the longest line greater than the average?

  Find, first in mm and then in cm, the length of a line which is:
11 $\frac{1}{2}$ of line **W**   12 3 times line **Y**
13 10 times line **Z**   14 $\frac{2}{5}$ of line **X**.

B

72 mm

The line above is 72 mm long.
Notice how the measurement is shown.

1 Carefully draw the line and put in the measurement.

Draw lines of the following lengths and show the measurement of each.
2 48 cm   3 86 mm   4 13 cm 4 mm
5 17.3 cm   6 146 mm   7 90 mm

C

100 cm = 1 metre   256 cm = 2.56 m
Notice that a point separates the metres from the centimetres.

Complete the following.
1 167 cm = ☐m ☐cm = ☐m
2 350 cm = ☐m ☐cm = ☐m
3   83 cm = ☐m ☐cm = ☐m
4 704 cm = ☐m ☐cm = ☐m
5 1092 cm = ☐m ☐cm = ☐m
6 1630 cm = ☐m ☐cm = ☐m

Write the following in cm.
7 5.79 m   8 12.70 m   9 9.08 m
10 24.34 m   11 31.02 m   12 40.05 m

How many cm are there in:
13 $\frac{1}{2}$ m   14 $\frac{1}{4}$ m   15 $\frac{3}{4}$ m   16 $1\frac{3}{4}$ m
17 $4\frac{1}{2}$ m 18 $3\frac{1}{4}$ m 19 $\frac{1}{100}$ m 20 $\frac{27}{100}$ m?

Which of these measurements are:
21 less than $\frac{1}{2}$ m   22 $\frac{1}{2}$ m or more?

| 0.68 m | 0.50 m | 0.47 m | 0.75 m |

Write the following measurements to the nearest metre.
23 3.72 m   24 2.09 m   25 3.50 m
26 482 cm   27 604 cm   28 890 cm

Measuring length mm cm m

A

10 mm = 1 cm	100 cm = 1 m

How many mm are there in:

1 10 cm   **2** 90 cm   **3** 80 cm

4 50 cm   **5** 30 cm   **6** 100 cm?

How many mm are there in:

7 2 m   **8** 5 m   **9** 8 m?

How many m are there in:

10 3000 mm   **11** 7000 mm   **12** 4000 mm

13 6000 mm   **14** 9000 mm   **15** 10 000 mm?

3234 mm = 3 m 234 mm = 3.234 m
3100 mm = 3 m 100 mm = 3.100 m

Notice that a point separates the metres from the millimetres.

Write and complete the following:

16 1462 mm = ☐ m ☐ mm = ☐ m

17 2709 mm = ☐ m ☐ mm = ☐ m

18 3048 mm = ☐ m ☐ mm = ☐ m

19 4006 mm = ☐ m ☐ mm = ☐ m

20 5350 mm = ☐ m ☐ mm = ☐ m

21 6090 mm = ☐ m ☐ mm = ☐ m.

Write the following as mm:

22 1.560 m   **27** 0.462 m

23 3.667 m   **28** 0.306 m

24 4.119 m   **29** 0.074 m

25 5.073 m   **30** 0.148 m

26 7.700 m   **31** 0.208 m.

B

The drawing shows a metre ruler much reduced in size.

Look at the drawing of the metre ruler.

What does one small division represent:

1 in cm   **2** in mm   **3** in m?

Write the length which each of the lines **V**, **W**, **X**, **Y** and **Z** represents:

4 in cm   **5** in mm   **6** in m.

Which of the lines represent:

7 less than half a metre

8 a half metre or more?

Write, first as cm, then as mm:

9 $\frac{1}{2}$ m   **10** $\frac{1}{4}$ m   **11** $\frac{3}{4}$ m.

Write each of the following to the nearest metre.

12 4700 mm   **13** 6650 mm   **14** 2050 mm

15 2883 mm   **16** 4449 mm   **17** 6501 mm

Write each of the following to the nearest half metre.
The drawing of the metre ruler will help you.

18 2100 mm   **19** 1600 mm   **20** 2950 mm

21 3300 mm   **22** 1880 mm   **23** 2450 mm

C

1 Measure in mm each of the lines below.

L

M

N

2 Write   **a** in mm   **b** in cm   **c** in m   the length of a line ten times the length of each of the lines **L**, **M**, and **N**.

Multiplication number and money

First work section **A**. Mark the answers and correct any mistakes.
Then do the same with sections **B, C, D, E** and **F**. Write the answers only.

A

1	93 ×4	2	70 ×6	3	35 ×5	4	56 ×7	5	78 ×8	6	67 ×9

1 93 ×4   2 70 ×6   3 35 ×5   4 56 ×7   5 78 ×8   6 67 ×9

7 66 ×7   8 42 ×6   9 37 ×8   10 89 ×2   11 85 ×9   12 45 ×7

Write the answers to the following, first as pence and then as £s.

B

1 27p ×3   2 48p ×2   3 12p ×7   4 13p ×6   5 18p ×4   6 14p ×7

7 19p ×3   8 37p ×2   9 14p ×5   10 12p ×8   11 16p ×6   12 9p ×9

Write the answers to the following as £s.

C

1 74p ×2   2 18p ×7   3 15p ×8   4 92p ×5   5 46p ×4   6 34p ×9

7 66p ×4   8 58p ×6   9 65p ×3   10 19p ×7   11 56p ×8   12 93p ×9

D

1 209 ×6   2 380 ×3   3 403 ×4   4 174 ×5   5 667 ×9   6 415 ×7

7 169 ×8   8 558 ×2   9 387 ×6   10 428 ×9   11 235 ×7   12 176 ×4

Write the answers to the following as £s.

E

1 £0·09 ×8   2 £0·07 ×7   3 £0·05 ×6   4 £0·15 ×4   5 £0·19 ×2   6 £0·25 ×3

7 £0·57 ×2   8 £0·14 ×9   9 £0·63 ×4   10 £0·58 ×5   11 £0·75 ×8   12 £0·26 ×7

F

1 £1·75 ×4   2 £9·50 ×2   3 £1·87 ×7   4 £9·05 ×3   5 £7·25 ×8   6 £5·90 ×9

7 £2·83 ×5   8 £6·46 ×6   9 £1·55 ×9   10 £6·87 ×3   11 £4·86 ×4   12 £3·96 ×8

Division number and money

First work section **A**. Mark the answers and correct any mistakes.
Then do the same with sections **B** to **G**. Write the answers only.

A

1 3)309	2 8)240	3 5)605	4 4)500	5 6)450	6 2)902
7 6)504	8 5)700	9 3)720	10 9)801	11 8)3200	12 7)7014

B

1 3)48p	2 7)91p	3 4)76p	4 2)58p	5 8)96p	6 6)78p
7 4)72	8 3)117	9 5)175	10 6)294	11 7)483	12 8)736
13 2)156	14 9)432	15 6)456	16 5)485	17 8)288	18 7)938

C

1 5)67p	2 8)83p	3 7)80p	4 9)85p	5 4)93p	6 6)92p
7 2)97	8 5)333	9 3)194	10 8)596	11 6)278	12 9)388
13 7)811	14 4)535	15 5)787	16 6)645	17 8)867	18 3)571

D Mixed examples.

1 2)57p	2 4)60p	3 3)70p	4 5)90p	5 8)91p	6 7)98p

E Write the answers as £s.

1 3)£0·87	2 6)£0·54	3 8)£0·64	4 9)£0·81	5 7)£0·63
6 4)£0·96	7 2)£0·78	8 3)£0·81	9 5)£0·75	10 8)£0·80

F

1 7)£3·29	2 6)£4·02	3 4)£3·00	4 2)£1·58	5 9)£3·96
6 3)£2·91	7 8)£7·12	8 5)£3·20	9 7)£6·16	10 4)£3·64

G

1 5)£6·65	2 8)£10·24	3 3)£5·61	4 4)£9·96	5 7)£10·08
6 8)£14·40	7 5)£8·05	8 7)£15·19	9 6)£12·48	10 9)£18·72

H Set down the following mixed examples. Check the answers by multiplying.
Then correct any mistakes.

1 7)845	2 2)£11·11	3 3)82p	4 5)£1·37	5 9)952
6 6)4248	7 8)£10·48	8 4)363	9 7)£9·83	10 9)5000

Number and money multiplication, division

A Multiply each of these numbers by 10.
1 39   2 405   3 830
4 21.8   5 30.5   6 109.6

Multiply each of these amounts by 10.
7 £0·15   8 £0·90   9 £1·10
10 £3·60   11 £5·56   12 £0·07
13 Find the product of 10 times 10 times 10.

Find the answer to each of the following by multiplying and then check by adding.
14 239 + 239 + 239 + 239
15 19p + 19p + 19p + 19p + 19p
16 £1·37 + £1·37 + £1·37

$\frac{1}{6}$ of a sum of money is 43p.
17 Find the sum of money.
18 What is the value of $\frac{5}{6}$ of the money?

Susan saved these coins.

> 5 FIFTIES, 3 TWENTIES, 4 TENS,
> 7 FIVES, 12 TWOS and 18 pennies.

19 Find her total savings.
20 She changed her savings for the least possible number of coins. Name the coins.

B Divide each of these numbers by 10.
1 890   2 5350   3 37
4 453   5 185   6 3042

Divide each of these amounts by 10.
7 £1·50   8 £12·00   9 £9·30
10 £8·00   11 £14·50   12 £55

Find the value of y when:
13 9y = 1908   14 7y = £8·26
15 6y = 714   16 8y = £10·00.
17 Six children shared a £5·00 prize equally. How much did each receive? How much money was left over?
18 What is the nearest whole number to 1000 which can be divided by 7 without a remainder?

Divide each of the numbers in the box:
19 by 6   20 by 8   21 by 9.

| a 288 | b 936 | c 1512 |

Find the numbers which, when multiplied by 7, will give these products.
22 98   23 161   24 721   25 2849
26 How many pamphlets costing 8p each can be bought for £1·84?

C

BROOKHILL SCHOOL

Class 1	Class 2	Class 3	Class 4	Class 5
24 children	30 children	27 children	30 children	29 children

1 Four exercise books were ordered for each child. How many was that for each class?
2 The books cost 5p each and the bill was for £28·00. How many books were ordered altogether?
3 Each class spent £13·50 on library books. How much did the library books cost altogether?
4 Find the **average** number of children in the classes by dividing the total number of children by the number of classes.

On Monday the following fraction of each class was absent.
Class 1 $\frac{1}{8}$ Class 2 $\frac{1}{5}$ Class 3 none
Class 4 $\frac{1}{6}$ Class 5 none
5 How many children were absent in each of the classes 1, 2 and 4?
6 How many children were absent altogether?
7 What fraction of the whole school was absent?
8 Every child in the school brought 8p to school for bus fares. Find the total amount they brought.

Money   shopping, change

A
Find the change from each of the given amounts. Write the answers only.

from a FIFTY	from £1	from a £5 note	from a £10 note
after spending	after spending	after spending	after spending
1 36p	6 45p	11 £2·36	16 £5·10
2 17p	7 72p	12 £3·44	17 £6·53
3 24p	8 39p	13 £1·28	18 £7·19
4 11p	9 63p	14 £0·92	19 £8·42
5 28p	10 26p	15 £4·06	20 £2·17

B

Special Offers

Jam	45p jar
Butter	56p pack
Cheese	98p 500 g
Plums	35p tin
Biscuits	27p pkt.

Find the cost of:
1 3 jars of jam
2 6 packs of butter
3 750 g of cheese
4 4 tins of plums
5 3 packets of biscuits.

6 Write and complete this bill.
                                £
    1½ kg cheese
    7 tins plums
    8 pkts. biscuits _____
                    Total
                    _____

7 Write three bills of your own.
   Ask your partner to check them.

C
Name the coins, using as few as possible, to pay for each of the following.
1 12 eggs at 7p each
2 5 lemons at 9p each
3 6 metres tape at 8p per m
4 200 g beef at £5·40 kg
5 4 loaves at 49p each
6 3 pkts. cornflakes at 61p pkt.
7 5 packets jelly at 15p pkt.
8 6 tins rice at 28p tin
9 1½ kg flour at 24p per kg

X
0·23
0·23
0·23
0·23
0·23
0·23

Y
0·36
0·36
0·36
0·36
0·36

Mother bought some tinned goods at the supermarket.
She was given bill **X**.
10 How many tins did she buy?   11 What was the price per tin?
12 Write the quickest way of finding the total cost.
Mother paid the bill with 3 FIFTIES.
13 How much change did she receive?

14 Look at bill **Y**. How many items were purchased?
15 Write the quickest way of finding the total cost.
16 If the bill was paid with £1, a FIFTY and 2 TWENTIES,
    how much change would there be?

D
Find the cost of one if:
1 10 cost 90p
2 10 cost 70p
3 10 cost 30p
4 10 cost £2·00
5 10 cost £1·20
6 10 cost £1·50
7 10 cost £3·70
8 10 cost £4·00
9 4 cost 96p
10 8 cost 72p
11 6 cost £1·50
12 5 cost £2·05.

Find the cost of:
13 10 if 1 costs £1·10
14 10 if 1 costs 18p
15 10 if 1 costs 11p
16 10 if 1 costs 23p
17 10 if 1 costs 32p
18 10 if 1 costs 45p
19 10 if 1 costs £1·30
20 10 if 1 costs £1·50
21 8 if 1 costs 22p
22 6 if 1 costs £1·20
23 5 if 1 costs 45p
24 4 if 1 costs £1·15.

Number the four rules, problems

A

1 Find the sum of 8, 9 and 7.

Multiply	2	5 by 9	3	3 by 8.
Divide	4	63 by 7	5	18 by 9.
Add	6	16 and 8	7	46 and 8.
Subtract	8	9 from 15	9	29 from 35.
Increase	10	7 by 9	11	57 by 9.
Decrease	12	14 by 8	13	94 by 8.

Find the product of:

14 7 and 7   15 9 and 36.

16 Find the difference between 6p and 13p.

Find the value of y in each of the following.

17 $7+y=12$
18 $y+y=14$
19 $y-6=13$
20 $y \times 4=36$
21 $y \div 5=5$
22 $\frac{1}{2}y=7$
23 $y+7+5=18$
24 $y-(8 \times 3)=17$
25 $(4 \times 9) \div y=6$
26 $y \div (5+4)=8$
27 $(y \times 7)=35$
28 $6 \times 3=y \times 2$
29 $y-3=4 \times 3$
30 $y \times y=81$
31 $y \times y \times y=8$
32 $\frac{y+y}{3}=4$

B

1 John had 15 cards. He lost 7 and won 9. How many had he then?

2 Peter had 8p. Tim had 5 times as much. How much had Tim?

3 James had 4 marbles. Neil and Richard each had 7. If they shared their marbles equally, how many would each have?

4 24p was divided so that Joan had one quarter and Claire had the remainder. How much did each have?

5 Rachael saved 7p each week for 7 weeks. Richard saved 9p for 6 weeks. Who saved more and by how much?

6 Football cards can be bought 3 for 8p. How many cards for 48p?

7 What distance is travelled in 4 hours at a speed of $8\frac{1}{2}$ km per hour?

8 In a game of darts, Ann scored 9, 9 and 7. Jane scored three 8's. How many more did Ann score than Jane?

9 Margaret has 56p. For how many days can she spend 7p each day?

10 David cuts 64 cm into 8 equal lengths. How long is each length?

11 9 children each received 6 sweets. How many sweets was that altogether?

12 Write the multiples of 6 between 40 and 58.

13 How many days are there in 6 weeks?

14 How many 7 metre lengths can be cut from 50 m?

15 Which two numbers have a product of 24 and a difference of 5?

16 Which numbers less than 50 can be divided exactly by both 6 and 8?

C

Write and complete using the signs >, < or = in place of ●.

1 $9+5 ● 5+9$
2 $9+1 ● 9 \times 1$
3 $6 \times 2 ● 4 \times 3$
4 $9 \div 1 ● 9-1$
5 $4 \times 6 ● 3 \times 8$
6 $7+9 ● 9+7$
7 $0 \times 3 ● 3 \times 0$
8 $9+8 ● 8+9$
9 $3+7 ● 7 \times 3$
10 $24 \div 6 ● 24 \div 4$
11 $21 \div 3 ● 21 \div 7$
12 $16 \div 8 ● 16-8$
13 $12 \div 6 ● 12-6$
14 $5 \times 5 ● 5+5$
15 $1+1 ● 1 \times 1$
16 $8 \times 5 ● 5 \times 8$

D

Write and complete using the signs $+, -, \times$ or $\div$ in place of ▲ or ■.

1 $(7▲1)■3=10$
2 $(6▲6)■6=30$
3 $(6▲9)■3=5$
4 $(9▲1)■5=14$
5 $6▲(8■2)=1$
6 $27▲(3■3)=3$
7 $17▲(5■3)=9$
8 $18▲(3■3)=3$
9 $(21▲3)■4=3$
10 $(5▲4)■6=7$
11 $(16▲4)■4=0$
12 $(18▲7)■5=5$
13 $48▲(12■4)=6$
14 $18▲(54■6)=9$
15 $42▲(6■1)=6$
16 $2▲(3■1)=8$

Prime numbers, multiples, factors, square numbers

A A number which has no factors other than itself and one is called a **prime number**.

7 is a prime number because it is only divisible by 7 and 1.
8 is not a prime number because it is divisible by 2 and 4, as well as by itself and 1.
Prime numbers can be found by using **Eratosthenes' Sieve**.

1 On squared paper, draw a 100 number square.
2 Cross out the number **1** in the number square.
3 Complete the sieve by taking out the multiples of the prime numbers 2, 3, 5 and 7 as follows.

Put a ring round the **2**. Then cross out all the multiples of 2. This has been done for you.

4 Put a ring round the **3**. Then cross out the multiples of 3.
5 Put a ring round the **5**. Then cross out the multiples of 5.
6 Put a ring round the **7**. Then cross out the multiples of 7.
7 Make a list of the numbers which are ringed or not crossed out. This is the set of prime numbers less than 100.

Eratosthenes was a Greek mathematician who lived about 2000 years ago.

B Write the following sets of multiples.
1 $S = \{$multiples of 4 between 41 and 61$\}$
2 $T = \{$multiples of 6 between 61 and 91$\}$
3 $U = \{$multiples of 8 between 81 and 111$\}$
4 $V = \{$multiples of 9 between 91 and 121$\}$
5 Copy and complete the chart of the factors of the numbers given.
Omit 1 and the number itself.
The first is done for you.

number	tables of				
	2	3	4	5	6
12	6×2	4×3	3×4		2×6
15					
18					
24					
30					

Which of the numbers listed in the table are multiples of both:
6 2 and 3   7 3 and 4   8 3 and 5
9 4 and 5   10 5 and 6   11 2, 3 and 4?
Write the factors of the following.
(Omit 1 and the number itself.)
12 36   13 40   14 48   15 60

C **A square number is the product of two equal factors.**
Study the diagrams below.

1

2 groups of 2
2×2

3 groups of 3
3×3

A short way of writing 2×2 is 2^2 which is read as 'two squared'.
Write and complete:
1 $3^2 = 3 \times 3 = \square$ 2 $4^2 = 4 \times 4 = \square$.
3 On squared paper, draw a diagram to show 5 squared 5^2.
4 Under the diagram write and complete:
$5^2 = 5 \times 5 = \square$.

The numbers 1, 4, 9, 16, 25 are called square numbers.
5 Write the next five square numbers.
Write and complete:
6 $64 = \square^2$ 7 $81 = \square^2$ 8 $100 = \square^2$.
Find the value of:
9 $3^2 + 1^2$ 10 $4^2 - 2^2$ 11 $5^2 + 10^2$
12 $10^2 - 9^2$ 13 $8^2 + 3^2$ 14 $6^2 + 5^2$.

Fractions

A

a whole one

The strip is a whole one, a fraction of which has been shaded.
The fraction shaded is **one-third** $\frac{1}{3}$.

$\frac{1}{3}$ The number **below** the line in the fraction tells you into how many equal parts the whole one is divided.
This number gives the name to the fraction and is called the **denominator** of the fraction.

Write these fractions in figures.
1 one-sixth   2 one-half   3 one-third
4 one-tenth   5 one-fifth   6 one-eighth

Write these fractions in words.
7 $\frac{1}{4}$ 8 $\frac{1}{7}$ 9 $\frac{1}{9}$ 10 $\frac{1}{20}$ 11 $\frac{1}{100}$

Each of the shapes below represents a whole one. Write in figures the fraction of each which is shaded.

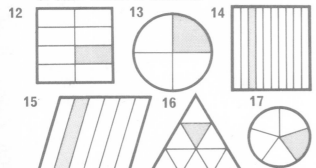

12   13   14
15   16   17

18 Look at the diagram, then write these fractions in order of size, the largest first.
$\frac{1}{6}$ $\frac{1}{4}$ $\frac{1}{3}$ $\frac{1}{8}$

a whole one			
$\frac{1}{4}$	$\frac{1}{4}$	$\frac{1}{4}$	$\frac{1}{4}$
$\frac{1}{8}$ $\frac{1}{8}$ $\frac{1}{8}$ $\frac{1}{8}$ $\frac{1}{8}$ $\frac{1}{8}$ $\frac{1}{8}$ $\frac{1}{8}$			
$\frac{1}{3}$	$\frac{1}{3}$	$\frac{1}{3}$	
$\frac{1}{6}$ $\frac{1}{6}$ $\frac{1}{6}$ $\frac{1}{6}$ $\frac{1}{6}$ $\frac{1}{6}$			

19 Write these fractions in order of size, the largest first. $\frac{1}{5}$ $\frac{1}{10}$ $\frac{1}{6}$ $\frac{1}{4}$
Write the denominator of each of these fractions.

20 $\frac{1}{2}$ 21 $\frac{1}{10}$ 22 $\frac{1}{20}$ 23 $\frac{1}{15}$

B

a whole one

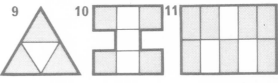

The strip is a whole one.
The fraction shaded is **three-eighths** $\frac{3}{8}$ of the whole one.

$\frac{3}{8}$ The number **above** the line in the fraction tells you how many of the parts have been taken.
This number is called the **numerator** of the fraction.

Write these fractions in figures.
1 seven-eighths   2 four-fifths
3 nine-tenths

Write these fractions in words.
4 $\frac{2}{7}$ 5 $\frac{5}{6}$ 6 $\frac{8}{9}$ 7 $\frac{7}{12}$ 8 $\frac{13}{100}$

Each of the shapes below represents a whole one.
Write in figures the fraction which is:
a shaded   b not shaded.

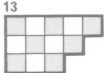

9   10   11
12   13   14

All the fractions you have written are **less than a whole one**.
These are called **proper fractions**.
Write all the proper fractions which have a denominator of:
15 3   16 5   17 8   18 10.

What fraction must be added to each of the following to make a whole one?
19 $\frac{2}{5}$ 20 $\frac{5}{8}$ 21 $\frac{9}{10}$ 22 $\frac{3}{20}$
23 $\frac{2}{3}$ 24 $\frac{1}{6}$ 25 $\frac{7}{12}$ 26 $\frac{6}{100}$

27 Write these fractions in order of size, the largest first.
$\frac{3}{8}$ $\frac{3}{4}$ $\frac{3}{12}$ $\frac{3}{7}$ $\frac{3}{10}$

Fractions

A

1 The sweets in a box are shared equally among 10 children. What fraction of the sweets does each child receive?

2 A sum of money is shared equally among 9 children. What fraction of the money does each child receive?

3 A number is divided by 7. What fraction of the number is the answer?

4 What fraction of 5 is a 3   b 4?

5 What fraction of 11 is a 4   b 7?

6 36 toffees were shared so that Jill had half of them, Mary had a quarter, Bill had a sixth and Lee had the remainder. How many did each have?

Find:

7 $\frac{1}{2}$ of a 78   b 54 cm c £1·50

8 $\frac{1}{3}$ of a 57   b 75p c £2·97

9 $\frac{1}{4}$ of a 96   b 84 cm c £2·40

10 $\frac{1}{5}$ of a 85   b 150 g c £2·00

11 $\frac{1}{6}$ of a 96   b 84p c £3·96

12 $\frac{1}{10}$ of a 170   b 250 m c £3·80.

13 Gary had 60 cards. He lost one-quarter of them. How many was that?

14 Peter and John each had 80p to spend. Peter spent $\frac{1}{5}$ of his money and John spent $\frac{1}{4}$ of his money. How much more did John spend than Peter?

$$£1·00 = 100p \qquad £\tfrac{1}{100} = 1p$$

15 What fraction of £1 is 1 penny?

16 Write: £$\frac{1}{100}$ = □p
    £$\frac{1}{10}$ = □p.

$$1 \text{ metre} = 100 \text{ cm} \qquad \tfrac{1}{100} \text{ m} = 1 \text{ cm}$$

17 What fraction of 1 m is 1 cm?

18 Write: $\frac{1}{100}$ m = □cm
    $\frac{1}{10}$ m = □cm.

What fraction is:

19 7p of £1   20 3p of £1

21 10p of £1   22 70p of £1

23 3 cm of 1 m   24 29 cm of 1 m?

B

1 A strip of paper is folded into 8 equal parts. If 5 of the parts are cut off, what fraction of the strip remains?

A cake is cut into 5 equal slices, 2 of which are eaten. What fraction of the cake:

2 is eaten   3 remains?

4 Write and complete: To find $\frac{2}{3}$ of a number or quantity, divide it into □ equal parts and take □ of the parts.

Describe in the same way how you would find:

5 $\frac{3}{4}$ of 96   6 $\frac{5}{8}$ of 64p   7 $\frac{2}{5}$ of 500 g. Write the answer in each case.

From a bag of 100 marbles, Robin took $\frac{7}{10}$ of them.

8 What fraction remained?

9 How many marbles did Robin take?

10 How many remained in the bag?

11 If Robin had only taken $\frac{3}{5}$ of the marbles, how many would he have had?

12 What fraction would remain?

Find:

13 $\frac{3}{4}$ of 36   22 $\frac{5}{6}$ of 240

14 $\frac{2}{3}$ of 48p   23 $\frac{9}{10}$ of 100

15 $\frac{5}{6}$ of 96   24 $\frac{3}{8}$ of £4·00

16 $\frac{3}{10}$ of £1·00   25 $\frac{3}{5}$ of 50p

17 $\frac{5}{8}$ of 24p   26 $\frac{3}{10}$ of £2·00

18 $\frac{3}{4}$ of 56   27 $\frac{7}{8}$ of 360

19 $\frac{2}{5}$ of 150 g   28 $\frac{3}{100}$ of £1·00

20 $\frac{2}{3}$ of 1 hour   29 $\frac{13}{100}$ of £1·00

21 $\frac{4}{5}$ of 90 cm   30 $\frac{52}{100}$ of £1·00.

Ann and Kate shared £1·20 so that Ann had $\frac{3}{8}$ of the money and Kate had the remainder.

31 What fraction of the money did Kate have?

32 How much money did each girl receive?

What fraction is:

33 5 kg of 12 kg   34 89p of £1

35 7 cm of 25 cm   36 3 ℓ of 10 ℓ?

Fractions

A The pie chart shows how Andrew spent one hour at school.

What fraction of the hour was spent on:
1 changing 2 games
3 dinner 4 reading?

One small division on the chart represents 5 min.
5 How long did it take him to have his dinner?

How many minutes were spent on:
6 changing 7 games 8 reading?

On a school outing, James spent £4·80. The pie chart shows how he spent it.

What fraction of the whole amount was spent on:
9 bus fares
10 the total of the other items?

How much did he spend on:
11 bus fares 12 the zoo
13 ice cream 14 food?

The diagram shows the different ways in which the children of Highgate School usually travel to school.

walk	cycle	bus	car

What fraction of the children travel by:
15 bus 16 cycle 17 car
18 walking to school?

If there are 200 children in the school, how many children:
19 travel by car 20 walk to school?

If there were 350 children in the school, how many would travel by:
21 cycle 22 bus?

Jill had £4. She spent $\frac{1}{4}$ of it on a book, $\frac{1}{8}$ on sweets, $\frac{3}{8}$ on a game and the remainder on a ball.
23 How much money did she spend on each item?

B Whole numbers with a fraction are called **mixed numbers**.

$$1 + \tfrac{3}{4} = 1\tfrac{3}{4}$$

$$1 + \tfrac{2}{3} = 1\tfrac{2}{3}$$

$$1 + \tfrac{4}{5} = 1\tfrac{4}{5}$$

1 How many quarters are there in $1\tfrac{3}{4}$?
Write: $1\tfrac{3}{4} = \tfrac{\square}{4}$.
2 How many thirds are there in $1\tfrac{2}{3}$?
Write: $1\tfrac{2}{3} = \tfrac{\square}{3}$.
3 How many fifths are there in $1\tfrac{4}{5}$?
Write: $1\tfrac{4}{5} = \tfrac{\square}{5}$.

Notice that in each of the answers the **numerator** is larger than the **denominator**. Such fractions are called **improper fractions**.

How many whole ones are there in:
4 8 quarters 5 9 thirds 6 40 tenths
7 24 eighths 8 20 fifths 9 42 sixths
10 $\tfrac{15}{3}$ 11 $\tfrac{28}{7}$ 12 $\tfrac{90}{9}$ 13 $\tfrac{15}{5}$?

Write the answers to the following as improper fractions. e.g. $1\tfrac{2}{3} = \tfrac{5}{3}$
How many eighths are there in:
14 $1\tfrac{5}{8}$ 15 2 16 $2\tfrac{3}{8}$ 17 $3\tfrac{7}{8}$?
How many fifths are there in:
18 $1\tfrac{2}{5}$ 19 6 20 $4\tfrac{3}{5}$ 21 $5\tfrac{4}{5}$?
How many tenths are there in:
22 $3\tfrac{3}{10}$ 23 5 24 $4\tfrac{9}{10}$ 25 $10\tfrac{7}{10}$?

Change these improper fractions to mixed numbers.
26 $\tfrac{17}{2}$ 27 $\tfrac{19}{8}$ 28 $\tfrac{27}{10}$ 29 $\tfrac{23}{5}$
30 $\tfrac{23}{6}$ 31 $\tfrac{25}{3}$ 32 $\tfrac{39}{4}$ 33 $\tfrac{18}{7}$

Change these mixed numbers to improper fractions.
34 $4\tfrac{1}{4}$ 35 $2\tfrac{1}{2}$ 36 $3\tfrac{3}{5}$ 37 $4\tfrac{1}{3}$
38 $5\tfrac{7}{10}$ 39 $6\tfrac{3}{8}$ 40 $8\tfrac{7}{10}$ 41 $7\tfrac{4}{7}$

Puzzle corner

A

1	2	3	4
5	6	7	8
9	10	11	12
13	14	15	16

From this number square find the following sets.
Use brackets in your answers.

1. S=a set of four square numbers
2. P=a set of five pairs of numbers each of which totals 11
3. T=a set of three pairs of numbers each of which totals 15

Find the total of the set of:

4. even numbers   5. odd numbers.

The diagonals of the square are shown by dotted lines.

6. Add the numbers on each diagonal. What do you find?

B

1. How many triangles, both large and small, are there in this rectangle?

The letter Y stands for an odd number.

Write the next odd number which is:

2. greater than Y   3. less than Y.

On one side of a street, a row of 15 houses is numbered 2, 4, 6 . . .
Find the number of:

4. the sixth house
5. the last but one house
6. the house in the middle of the row.

Write and complete these series.

7. 8 4 2 1 ☐ ☐
8. 1000 100 10 ☐ ☐ $\frac{1}{100}$
9. $\frac{3}{4}$ $1\frac{1}{2}$ $2\frac{1}{4}$ 3 ☐ ☐

C

1		15	
8	11		5
	7		9
13			16

1. Copy the diagram and write in the numbers shown.
   It is the magic square of 16. The numbers in each column, each row and from corner to corner must add up to 34.
2. Complete your diagram. It should contain all the numbers from 1 to 16.

   There are 15 other ways of arranging these numbers so that they add up to 34 in every direction.
3. See if you can find one way for yourself.

D

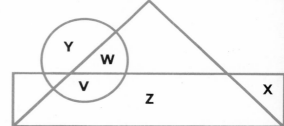

In the diagram there is a rectangle, a circle and a triangle.

1. Which letter is in the rectangle only?
2. Which letter is in both the triangle and the circle, but not in the rectangle?
3. Which letter is in all three shapes?
4. Find two numbers the sum of which is 16 and the product 63.
5. Find two numbers with a difference of 8 and a product of 65.
6. Find two numbers with a total of 20 and a difference of 6.

$$19+19+19+19=76$$

Now write the answers only.

7. 76−19−19−19−19   8. 19×4
9. 4×19   10. 76÷4   11. 76÷19

Lines and angles

A

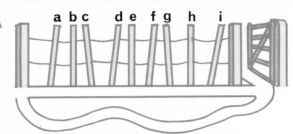

There are two paths from the corner post to the gate.

1 Which is shorter, the straight path or the curved one?

2 Give a reason for your answer.
Some of the posts on the fence are not upright.
Name the posts which you think are:

3 vertical   4 oblique.

5 Use a set square to find which of the posts are at right angles to the ground.

6 Draw a long horizontal line **XY**.

7 Place a set square on the line and draw a line at right angles to it.

8 Now move the set square along the line **XY** and draw more lines at right angles to it.

> **Remember**
> When a line is at right angles to another line, it is **perpendicular** to it.

9 Draw four perpendiculars on the other side of the line **XY**.

B

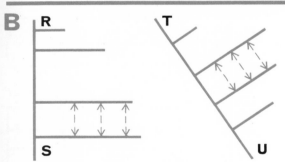

1 Draw a long vertical line **RS**.

2 Place a set square on the line and draw four lines of different lengths perpendicular to it.

3 Measure the distance between two of the lines at different points, as shown in the diagram.

4 What do you find?

5 Draw a long oblique line **TU**.

6 Draw four lines of different lengths perpendicular to it.

7 Check, by measuring, that the distance between a pair of the lines is always the same.

8 Look around the class-room and see how many perpendiculars you can find. Work with a partner, checking each other.

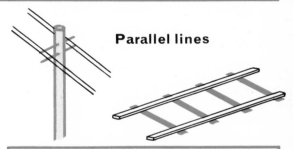

Parallel lines

> Lines which are the same distance apart throughout their length are called **parallel lines.**

Look again at the perpendiculars you have drawn.
Are they parallel on:

9 the horizontal line **XY**

10 the vertical line **RS**

11 the oblique line **TU**?

12 Place your ruler horizontally on a sheet of paper and draw a line along each edge of the ruler. These lines are parallel. How do you know this?

In the same way, use your ruler to draw:

13 three vertical parallel lines

14 three oblique parallel lines.

15 Draw three curved lines that are parallel.

Measuring length mm cm m km

A

Peter's height is $1\frac{1}{2}$ metres.

His brother is 37 cm taller and his sister is 19 cm shorter.

Find the height in cm of:

1 Peter's brother

2 Peter's sister.

Peter's father is 1 m 80 cm tall.

3 How much taller is he than Peter?

4 By how many cm is Peter's father taller than Uncle Richard who is $1\frac{3}{4}$ m tall?

5 Write the length of this rod in cm.

6 Find the length in m of ten such rods.

B

1 James estimates the length of a plank of wood to be 3 metres. Its actual length is 276 cm. By how many cm is his estimate too long or too short?

Mother wishes to make a pair of curtains each 147 cm long.

2 Find in cm the total length she requires.

3 Now write the answer to the nearest m.

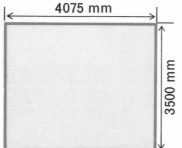

This is a plan of a room.

Write each measurement:

4 in metres

5 to the nearest m.

6 By how many mm is the length of the room greater than its width?

Which is the greater length and by how much? Write the answers in mm.

7 $\frac{3}{4}$ m or 800 mm   8 30 cm or 290 mm

9 $6\frac{1}{2}$ m or 6250 mm   10 495 cm or 5 m

Write the answers in mm.

11 $\frac{1}{2}$ m+230 mm   12 $\frac{1}{4}$ m+225 mm

13 $\frac{3}{4}$ m−150 mm   14 1 m−$\frac{3}{4}$ m

C

Lengths are usually measured in metres or millimetres.

Write the answers to the following, first in mm and then in m.

1 102 mm+79 mm+85 mm

2 656 mm+735 mm+207 mm

3 3 m−389 mm   5 208 mm×9

4 $1\frac{1}{2}$ m−96 mm   6 $\frac{1}{3}$ of 864 mm

Write the answers to the following, first in m and then in mm.

7 2.390 m+1.085 m+0.647 m

8 3.072 m−1.093 m

9 3.065 m×4   11 $\frac{1}{4}$ of 1.856 m

10 2.760 m×6   12 $\frac{1}{10}$ of 20.08 m

D

Longer distances, e.g. between towns, are measured in **kilometres km**.

Speeds are measured in **kilometres per hour km/h**.

1 kilometre = 1000 metres

Find how many m there are in:

1 $\frac{1}{2}$ km   2 $\frac{1}{4}$ km   3 $\frac{3}{4}$ km.

4 Copy and complete the table by filling in the empty spaces.

m	km	m	km
1200			
	2	750	
			3.400
	8	500	
5750			
	10	250	

Write each of the following to the nearest kilometre.

5 3950 m   6 9460 m   7 15 500 m

8 7390 m   9 12 500 m   10 6450 m

Write each of the following to the nearest half kilometre.

11 1600 m   12 2950 m   13 5450 m

14 1180 m   15 3185 m   16 8695 m

How far will a car travel at 60 km/h in:

17 30 min   18 15 min   19 45 min

20 10 min   21 5 min   22 1 min?

Graphs

A

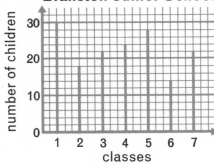

The graph shows the number of children in each of the classes in Branston Junior School.

From the graph, find what is shown on:
1 the vertical axis
2 the horizontal axis.

Without counting, write:
3 the class which is the largest
4 the class which is the smallest
5 the classes in which there are less than 26 children
6 the two classes in which there are the same number of children.

Look at the number scale on the vertical axis.
7 How many children are represented by one division?

Using the same scale, how many children would be represented by:
8 3 divisions
9 5½ divisions?

How many divisions would represent:
10 8 children
11 13 children?

12 Look at the graph again and then copy and complete this table.

class	1	2	3	4	5	6	7
number of children							

The table below shows the number of children who were absent from school during one week.

day	Mon.	Tues.	Wed.	Thurs.	Fri.
number absent	18	24	28	15	21

13 On squared paper, using the same scale, draw a graph to show the number of children who were absent each day.

B

When deciding which scale to mark on the axis of a graph, make sure the scale fits the numbers which have to be represented.

Here are four different scales.

scale A	scale B	scale C	scale D
150	120	90	300
125	100	75	250
100	80	60	200
75	60	45	150
50	40	30	100
25	20	15	50
0	0	0	0

By counting, find how many are represented by one division on:
1 scale A
2 scale B
3 scale C
4 scale D.

There are two lines drawn on each scale. Find the number each line represents on:
5 scale A
6 scale B
7 scale C
8 scale D.

Find from the scales how many divisions represent the following.

scale A	9	35	10	65	11	95
scale B	12	16	13	52	14	84
scale C	15	15	16	36	17	63
scale D	18	70	19	160	20	215

Graphs

A

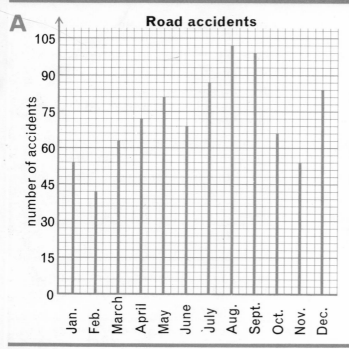

Road accidents

number of accidents

The graph shows the number of road accidents in a town for every month of a year.

In which month were there:
1 the most accidents
2 the least accidents?

In which months were there:
3 70 or more accidents
4 60 accidents or less?

5 Draw two columns. Write the months of the year in one and the number of accidents monthly in the other.

6 Check the answers.

7 In which of the three-monthly periods below were there the most accidents? Give a reason for this.

a Jan., Feb., March b April, May, June

c July, Aug., Sept. d Oct., Nov., Dec.

B

Jane and Peter made a count of traffic passing the school.
They made this record sheet, on which they marked the different kinds of vehicles.

vehicles	number counted
buses	⊬⊬ ⊬⊬ ⊬⊬ ⊬⊬ ///
cars	⊬⊬ ⊬⊬ ⊬⊬ ⊬⊬ ⊬⊬ ⊬⊬ ⊬⊬ ⊬⊬ ⊬⊬ ⊬⊬ ⊬⊬ ⊬⊬ ⊬⊬ ⊬⊬ ⊬⊬
motor cycles	⊬⊬ ⊬⊬ ⊬⊬ ⊬⊬ ⊬⊬ ⊬⊬ ///
other vehicles	⊬⊬ ⊬⊬ ⊬⊬ ⊬⊬ ⊬⊬ ⊬⊬ ⊬⊬ ⊬⊬ ⊬⊬ ⊬⊬ /

Then they made this graph.

Traffic count

buses
cars
motor cycles
other vehicles

0   10   20   30   40   50   60   70   80
number of vehicles

1 On which axis is the number of vehicles shown?

2 What is the scale used?

3 Of which type of vehicle was there
  a the most   b the least?

4 How many of each type of vehicle passed the school? Check the answers.

5 On squared paper, draw the graph again but let one division represent 3 vehicles.

6 Draw a record sheet and with a partner make a similar count of the traffic which passes along a main road in 15 minutes.

7 Choose a suitable scale and draw a graph of the count.

Number facts +, −, ×, ÷, money

Place a strip of paper alongside test **A** and write the answers only.
Then go on to tests **B**, **C**, **D** and **E**. Look carefully at the signs.
Try to beat the clock. Time 7½ min Mark the answers and correct any mistakes.

A		**B**		**C**		**D**		**E**	
1	4+7	1	15−9	1	3×6	1	25÷5	1	1×9
2	9+5	2	12−7	2	4×5	2	0÷4	2	64÷8
3	3+8	3	12−3	3	8×7	3	36÷6	3	7×7
4	8+9	4	16−8	4	3×4	4	42÷7	4	24÷8
5	7+7	5	18−9	5	6×6	5	56÷8	5	9×6
6	5+6	6	14−8	6	9×9	6	8÷8	6	0÷7
7	8+6	7	12−6	7	8×2	7	30÷5	7	8×4
8	2+9	8	13−4	8	4×7	8	49÷7	8	81÷9
9	7+5	9	11−3	9	5×8	9	28÷4	9	3×9
10	6+9	10	11−9	10	6×4	10	16÷8	10	18÷2
11	8+4	11	13−6	11	9×2	11	24÷6	11	8×6
12	9+9	12	17−8	12	7×9	12	21÷7	12	63÷9
13	6+6	13	15−7	13	3×7	13	32÷4	13	7×2
14	8+8	14	11−4	14	6×5	14	48÷8	14	54÷9
15	9+7	15	14−9	15	9×4	15	72÷9	15	2×5
16	5+8	16	13−5	16	8×8	16	36÷9	16	14÷7
17	9+3	17	11−6	17	7×5	17	6÷6	17	9×8
18	8+7	18	12−8	18	3×8	18	45÷9	18	18÷6
19	4+9	19	14−7	19	6×7	19	40÷8	19	0×3
20	6+7	20	16−9	20	5×9	20	35÷7	20	27÷9

F Find the total value of the money in each of the rows.

	50	20	10	5	2	1
1	2		3	6	5	5
2	3	2		2	6	7
3	4	2	4	8	9	8
4	5	3	1	10	8	5
5	10	1	3	7	7	9
6	7	5	10	5	4	5

How many TENS would be given for:

7 15 TWOS, 35 pennies and 3 FIVES
8 9 FIVES, 9 TWOS and 7 pennies
9 28 TWOS, 3 FIVES and 9 pennies
10 13 FIVES, 12 TWOS and 1 penny?

G Find the change from each amount given.

	amount given	amount spent
1	a FIFTY	27p
2	£1	64p
3	2 TWENTIES	36p
4	1 TWENTY and 1 TEN	22p
5	3 FIVES	9p
6	a FIFTY and 1 TWENTY	63p
7	2 TENS and 3 FIVES	32p
8	2 FIVES and 4 TWOS	17p
9	1 TWENTY	15p
10	a FIFTY	33p
11	4 TENS	34p
12	a TEN and a FIVE	11p
13	a FIFTY	16p

Making sure

A

Set down and work the following.

1 £12·09+£5·27+£9·60
2 £1·35+76p+19p
3 £2·94+£0·08+36p
4 £12·77−£9·89
5 £33·00−£26·53
6 £43·22−£17·25

7 £0·59×7
8 £12·65×3
9 £5·50×8
10 £0·78×2
11 £1·30×10
12 £8·75×4

13 £16·40÷5
14 £17·52÷6
15 £90·81÷9
16 £31·32÷4
17 £15·19÷7
18 £16·72÷8

B

Write the answers as decimals.

1 $\frac{26}{10}$
2 $\frac{43}{10}$
3 $\frac{104}{10}$
4 $\frac{305}{10}$

5 $300+60+5+\frac{3}{10}$
6 $1000+800+7+\frac{7}{10}$
7 $500+10+\frac{1}{10}$
8 $2000+9+\frac{2}{10}$

Write the answers as decimals.

9 $4\frac{7}{10}+1\frac{4}{10}$
10 $3\frac{1}{4}+2\frac{1}{4}$
11 $4-\frac{9}{10}$
12 $8\frac{1}{4}-7\frac{3}{4}$

13 $3\frac{6}{10}+1\frac{8}{10}$
14 $8\frac{7}{10}+\frac{1}{2}$
15 $3-1\frac{2}{10}$
16 $5-\frac{1}{5}$

17 $9\frac{9}{10}+4\frac{3}{10}$
18 $6\frac{1}{2}+\frac{3}{10}$
19 $7-1\frac{7}{10}$
20 $2-1\frac{2}{5}$

Write and complete the following.

21 2.847m = ☐ m☐mm = ☐mm
22 4.096m = ☐ m☐mm = ☐mm
23 1.803m = ☐ m☐mm = ☐mm

Write the following as mm.

24 1.250 m   25 2.058 m   26 0.875 m

Write answers only to the following.

27 189 mm+235 mm+243 mm=☐ mm
28 1 m−382 mm=☐ mm   29 2 m−1$\frac{1}{4}$ m=☐ mm
30 409 mm×9=☐ m   31 3.167 m×3=☐ m
32 10 m÷8=☐ m   33 8.750 m÷10=☐ m

C

Measure each of the lines and write the answers **a** in mm **b** in cm **c** to the nearest cm.

1
2
3
4
5

6 Which of these pairs of lines are parallel lines?

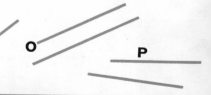

J   K   L   M   N   O   P

D

Write the fraction of each shape below which is **a** shaded **b** unshaded.

1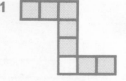
2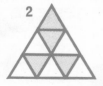
3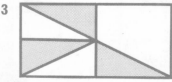
4
5

Find:

6 $\frac{3}{4}$ of £1·20
7 $\frac{5}{6}$ of 960 mm
8 $\frac{7}{10}$ of 1 km
9 $\frac{2}{5}$ of £1·00.

10 Write four fractions each with a different prime number less than 10 as a denominator.

Measuring mass

A These measures of mass are usually supplied with school scales.

1 Get the school scales and measures.
2 Feel the mass of 1 kg in your hand.
3 Get two piles of books of different sizes. Estimate a mass of 1 kg from each pile.
4 Use the scales and the 1 kg measure to find if your estimate is greater or less than 1 kg.

1 kilogram kg	=	1000 grams g

5 Hold in turn the 500 g, the 200 g and the 100 g measures in your hand.
Feel the mass of each.
6 Put into a bag a quantity of sand which you think has a mass of 500 g.
7 Use the scales and the 500 g measure to find if your estimate is greater or less than 500 g.
8 Make the mass of sand exactly 500 g.

In the same way, using sand, estimate and then measure a mass of:
9 200 g   10 100 g.

B Find how many:
1 medium-sized potatoes have a mass of $\frac{1}{2}$ kg
2 marbles have a mass of 100 g
3 sheets of exercise paper have a mass of 50 g
4 drawing-pins have a mass of 100 g.
5 Practise with a partner estimating the mass of articles up to 1 kg.
6 Use the scales to find if each of your estimates is greater or less than the correct mass.

C By how many g is each of the following masses less than 1 kg?
1 930 g   2 640 g   3 280 g
4 750 g   5 895 g   6 90 g

By how many g is each of the following masses less than $\frac{1}{2}$ kg?
7 420 g   8 370 g   9 160 g
10 250 g   11 495 g   12 40 g

Write as a decimal fraction of 1 kg:
13 100 g   14 300 g   15 500 g
16 200 g   17 600 g   18 800 g.

How many grams are there in:
19 0.4 kg   20 0.7 kg   21 0.9 kg?

Look at the pictures of the parcels below.

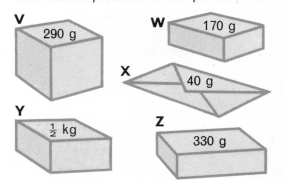

22 Find the difference in mass between the heaviest and the lightest parcel.
23 Which two parcels together have a mass of $\frac{1}{2}$ kg?
24 Which three parcels have a mass of 500 g?
25 Which two parcels together have the same mass as parcel **Z**?

Find the total mass of parcels:
26 **X, Y** and **Z**.   27 **V, W** and **Y**.
28 Find, in kg and g, the total mass of all the parcels.

A mass of 1 gram is too small to use as a measure in shops. Ask your teacher to show you a 1 g mass.
Some plastic cubes have a mass of 1 g.
29 Using the answer to **B4**, find how many drawing-pins have a mass of 10 g, 1g.

Measuring mass

A

1. You must learn to estimate masses greater than 1 kg. Get measures which have a total mass of 2 kg. Hold the mass in your hand and get the feel of it.
2. Put into a bag a quantity of sand which you think has a mass of 2 kg.
3. Use the scales and find if your estimate is greater or less than 2 kg.
4. Then, by adding or taking away sand, make its mass exactly 2 kg.
5. Draw this table.

article	estimated mass	actual mass	estimate >,< or = the actual mass
brick			
parcel of books			
4 large stones in a bag			
a packet of paper			

6. Collect the articles named in the list and estimate the mass of each to $\frac{1}{2}$ kg.
7. Use the sign >, < or = to show how accurate your estimates are.
8. Many goods, e.g. tinned vegetables, fruit and meat, have the mass of the contents printed on their labels. This is called the **net mass**. Ask mother if you may estimate the net mass in the tins and then check your accuracy from the labels.
9. Practise estimating the mass of other articles both large and small. Keep a record of your work.

B

How many grams are there in:
1. 2 kg
2. 5 kg
3. 7 kg
4. $3\frac{1}{2}$ kg
5. $8\frac{1}{2}$ kg
6. $\frac{1}{4}$ kg?

How many kg are there in:
7. 6000 g
8. 4000 g
9. 9000 g
10. 1500 g
11. 2500 g
12. 3250 g?

> 1250 g = 1 kg 250 g = 1.250 kg

Notice that a point separates the kilograms from the grams.

Write and complete the following.
13. 2560 g = ☐ kg ☐ g = ☐ kg
14. 3870 g = ☐ kg ☐ g = ☐ kg
15. 4095 g = ☐ kg ☐ g = ☐ kg
16. 8900 g = ☐ kg ☐ g = ☐ kg
17. 460 g = ☐ kg ☐ g = ☐ kg
18. 700 g = ☐ kg ☐ g = ☐ kg

C

Write the following as kg and g, then as kg.
1. 3050 g
2. 5880 g
3. 1740 g
4. 1800 g
5. 2250 g
6. 4050 g
7. 540 g
8. 350 g
9. 490 g

Write the following as grams.
10. 1.670 kg
11. 0.310 kg
12. 2.250 kg
13. 9.595 kg
14. 0.440 kg
15. 0.780 kg

How many grams are there in:
16. 3.2 kg
17. 2.6 kg
18. 3.9 kg
19. 1.4 kg
20. 0.8 kg
21. 6.1 kg
22. 5.5 kg
23. 3.3 kg
24. 4.7 kg?

Write the value in g of each of the figures underlined.
25. 2.2_4_6 kg
26. 3._8_70 kg
27. 2.13_5_ kg
28. _4_.113 kg
29. 5.31_8_ kg
30. 5._9_00 kg

Find the following totals in kg.
31. 460 g + 800 g + 550 g
32. 4.6 kg + 375 g

Measuring mass

A When goods are not pre-packed, scales of different types are used to find the mass.

You must learn to read the different dials on which pointers show the mass.

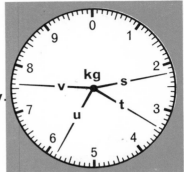

1 What is the greatest mass which can be shown on the dial in this picture?

2 What mass in grams does each small division represent?

3 Read the masses in kg and g shown by the pointers **s, t, u** and **v.**

4 Now write each of the masses in g and then in kg.

What mass must be added to make:

5 pointer **s** read $2\frac{1}{2}$ kg
6 pointer **t** read 4 kg
7 pointer **u** read $6\frac{1}{2}$ kg
8 pointer **v** read 8 kg?

B

1 What is the greatest mass in g which can be shown on this dial?

2 What mass does each small division represent?

Read the mass shown by each of the pointers **w, x, y** and **z** and then write each mass:

3 as g
4 as kg.

5 How many g less than 1 kg is shown by pointer **y**?

6 How many g more than $\frac{1}{2}$ kg is shown by pointer **z**?

C Write and complete using the sign > or < in place of ● .

1 370 g ● $\frac{1}{2}$ kg
2 650 g ● $\frac{1}{2}$ kg
3 905 g ● $\frac{1}{2}$ kg
4 190 g ● $\frac{1}{2}$ kg
5 480 g ● $\frac{1}{2}$ kg
6 550 g ● $\frac{1}{2}$ kg

Write each of the following to the nearest kg.

7 3600 g
8 5400 g
9 2750 g
10 3050 g
11 4080 g
12 6520 g

Write each of the following to the nearest $\frac{1}{2}$ kg.

13 3200 g
14 2700 g
15 1850 g
16 4300 g
17 5050 g
18 2600 g

Write the answers in kg.

19 150 g × 10
20 230 g × 7
21 9 kg ÷ 6
22 8 kg ÷ 5
23 380 g × 5
24 265 g × 6
25 7 kg ÷ 2
26 2 kg ÷ 8
27 750 g × 2
28 245 g × 4
29 10 kg ÷ 4
30 9 kg ÷ 10

D 1 kg costs 80p. Find the cost of:

1 500 g
2 250 g
3 100 g.

1 kg costs £1·20. Find the cost of:

4 500 g
5 750 g
6 200 g.

$\frac{1}{2}$ kg costs 70p. Find the cost of:

7 100 g
8 400 g
9 900 g.

$\frac{1}{2}$ kg costs £1. Find the cost of:

10 750 g
11 5 kg
12 $1\frac{1}{2}$ kg.

250 g of butter costs 26p. What is the cost of:

13 $\frac{1}{2}$ kg
14 $\frac{3}{4}$ kg
15 $1\frac{1}{2}$ kg?

16 100 g of steak costs 36p. Find the price of 900 g.

A joint of meat has a mass of $1\frac{1}{2}$ kg and costs £3·60. Find the cost of:

17 $\frac{1}{2}$ kg
18 100 g
19 300 g
20 700 g
21 250 g
22 450 g.

Measuring liquids

A

> The amount of liquid which a container holds is its capacity.

**The standard measure of liquids
is 1 litre (ℓ).**

1 Get various empty containers, e.g.
a milk bottle   a wine bottle
a large jar   a bowl
a bucket   a large jug.

Use the litre and half-litre measures to
find which of the containers hold:

2 less than ½ litre
3 1 litre approximately   4   more than 1 litre.
Keep a record of your work.

5 Get a medicine bottle, a cup and an egg-cup. Fill the medicine bottle with water.
How many bottlefuls are needed to fill the half-litre measure?

6 Now find how many   a   cupfuls   b   egg-cupfuls are needed to fill the ½-litre measure.

B

> **1 litre ℓ   =   1000 millilitres mℓ**

The pictures
show a 200 mℓ
and a 100 mℓ
measure.

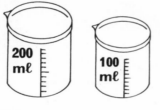

1 What does one small division on the
200 mℓ measure represent?

2 What does one small division on the
100 mℓ measure represent?

How many mℓ are there in:
3 $\frac{1}{2}$ ℓ   4 $\frac{1}{4}$ ℓ   5 $\frac{3}{4}$ ℓ?

6 How many times must you fill the
200 mℓ measure to make 1 litre?

7 What fraction of 1 litre is 200 mℓ?

Estimate the capacity in mℓ of:
8 the medicine bottle   9   the cup.
Check your estimates with a measure.

A useful measure for small containers is
the 5 mℓ medicine spoon.

10 Estimate the capacity in mℓ of the egg-
cup and check your estimate using a
medicine spoon.

C

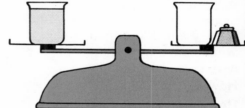

1 Get two litre measures, each having the
same mass.

2 Place one of the empty measures on a
pan of the scales.

3 Carefully pour 1 litre of water into the
other litre measure and place it on the
other pan of the scales.

4 Use the measures of mass to find the
mass of 1 litre of water.

5 Think of another way of finding the mass
of a litre of water.

You should find that:
**1 litre 1000 mℓ of water has
a mass of 1 kg 1000 g.**

6 Check your answer by measuring the
mass of different amounts of water,
e.g. half litre, 200 mℓ and then finding the
mass of a litre.

24-hour clock

24-hour clock times are used in bus, railway and airline timetables to show times of arrival and departure.

The 24-hour clock numbers the hours from 0 to 24, that is for **the whole day from midnight to midnight**. Neither a.m. nor p.m. is used when writing 24-hour clock times.

Remember   Use four figures when writing 24-hour clock times, the first two for **hours,** the last two after the point for **minutes past the hour**.

Times between midnight and midday

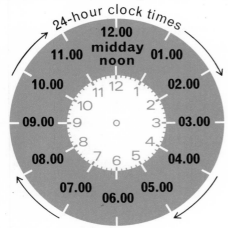

Look at the diagram above.

> The times in the outer coloured band show 24-hour clock times **before noon** (morning times).

Examples   8.00 a.m. is written 08.00
6.30 a.m. is written 06.30

Times between midday and midnight

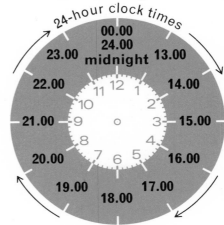

Look at the diagram above.

> The times in the outer coloured band show 24-hour clock times **after noon** (afternoon or evening times).

Examples   2.00 p.m. is written 14.00
7.30 p.m. is written 19.30

B Write these times as 24-hour clock times.

1 1.00 a.m.   **2** 4.00 a.m.   **3** 7.00 a.m.
4 3.00 p.m.   **5** 11.00 p.m.   **6** 5.00 p.m.
7 12.00 noon   **8** 12.00 midnight
9 Write a rule for changing p.m. times to 24-hour clock times.

Change to 24-hour clock times:

10 3.30 a.m.   **11** 4.15 p.m.   **12** 8.15 a.m.
13 1.30 p.m.   **14** 5.45 a.m.   **15** 10.45 p.m.
16 11.40 a.m.   **17** 6.25 p.m.   **18** 9.05 a.m.

Change these a.m. times to 24-hour clock times.

19 10 min past 3   **20** 25 min past 10
21 quarter to 7   **22** 5 min to 12

C Change these p.m. times to 24-hour clock times.

1 20 past 12   **2** half past 4
3 quarter to 9   **4** 10 min to 10
5 25 min to 8   **6** 6 min to 12

Change these 24-hour clock times to 12-hour clock times.
Remember to write a.m. or p.m.

7 19.00   **13** 03.10   **19** 20.04
8 06.00   **14** 15.15   **20** 00.10
9 14.00   **15** 09.30   **21** 02.28
10 02.00   **16** 17.05   **22** 16.45
11 18.00   **17** 23.06   **23** 06.16
12 05.00   **18** 08.20   **24** 13.25

Time

A

British airways shuttle service

Depart	Arrive
London	**Edinburgh**
07.40	**08.50**

Depart	Arrive
Edinburgh	**London**
07.40	**08.50**

London and Edinburgh

Departure times from London and Edinburgh both commence at 07.40.

Planes leave both airports at two-hourly intervals until 21.40.

Write in 24-hour clock times:

1. the departure time of each plane from London
2. the arrival time in Edinburgh of each plane.

Write in 12-hour clock times:

3. the departure time of each plane from Edinburgh
4. the arrival time in London of each plane.

Mark and correct your answers to questions **1** to **4**.

5. What is the arrival time in Edinburgh of the first plane after 3.00 p.m.?
6. What is the departure time from Edinburgh of the first plane after 5.45 p.m.?
7. At what time must a man leave London by shuttle service in order to arrive in Edinburgh by 2.30 p.m.?
8. What is the latest flight from Edinburgh, on which Mr McBride can travel, to arrive in London by 1.30 p.m.?
9. Give the time of departure of his first return flight after 6.00 p.m.

B

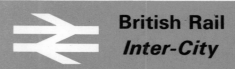

British Rail
Inter-City

London and Birmingham

Outward journey	
London (Euston)	dep. **09.10**
Birmingham (New Street)	arr. **10.43**

Return journey	
Birmingham (New Street)	dep. **17.48**
London (Euston)	arr. **19.22**

Mr Brown travels by *Inter-City* from London to Birmingham and back again in a day.
His train times are shown above.

Write in 12-hour clock times the departure time from:

1. London
2. Birmingham.

Write in 12-hour clock times the arrival time at:

3. Birmingham
4. London.

Find in hours and minutes how long:

5. the outward journey takes
6. the return journey takes.

7. Which is the quicker journey and by how many minutes?

Find in hours and minutes the time:

8. Mr Brown spends in Birmingham
9. Mr Brown spends in the train.

Mr Brown allows 50 minutes to travel between his London home and the station.

10. At what time does he leave home in the morning?
11. At what time does he arrive home in the evening?
12. For how long is Mr Brown away from home?

Time the calendar

	January	February	March		April	May	June
Mon.	4 11 18 25	1 8 15 22	1 8 15 22 29	Mon.	5 12 19 26	3 10 17 24 31	7 14 21 28
Tues.	5 12 19 26	2 9 16 23	2 9 16 23 30	Tues.	6 13 20 27	4 11 18 25	1 8 15 22 29
Wed.	6 13 20 27	3 10 17 24	3 10 17 24 31	Wed.	7 14 21 28	5 12 19 26	2 9 16 23 30
Thur.	7 14 21 28	4 11 18 25	4 11 18 25	Thur.	1 8 15 22 29	6 13 20 27	3 10 17 24
Fri.	1 8 15 22 29	5 12 19 26	5 12 19 26	Fri.	2 9 16 23 30	7 14 21 28	4 11 18 25
Sat.	2 9 16 23 30	6 13 20 27	6 13 20 27	Sat.	3 10 17 24	1 8 15 22 29	5 12 19 26
Sun.	3 10 17 24 31	7 14 21 28	7 14 21 28	Sun.	4 11 18 25	2 9 16 23 30	6 13 20 27

	July	August	September		October	November	December
Mon.	5 12 19 26	2 9 16 23 30	6 13 20 27	Mon.	4 11 18 25	1 8 15 22 29	6 13 20 27
Tues.	6 13 20 27	3 10 17 24 31	7 14 21 28	Tues.	5 12 19 26	2 9 16 23 30	7 14 21 28
Wed.	7 14 21 28	4 11 18 25	1 8 15 22 29	Wed.	6 13 20 27	3 10 17 24	1 8 15 22 29
Thur.	1 8 15 22 29	5 12 19 26	2 9 16 23 30	Thur.	7 14 21 28	4 11 18 25	2 9 16 23 30
Fri.	2 9 16 23 30	6 13 20 27	3 10 17 24	Fri.	1 8 15 22 29	5 12 19 26	3 10 17 24 31
Sat.	3 10 17 24 31	7 14 21 28	4 11 18 25	Sat.	2 9 16 23 30	6 13 20 27	4 11 18 25
Sun.	4 11 18 25	1 8 15 22 29	5 12 19 26	Sun.	3 10 17 24 31	7 14 21 28	5 12 19 26

Answer the following questions. When necessary use the calendar to help you.

How many:
days in a week

2 weeks in a year   3 months in a year?

List the months in which there are:
4 30 days   5 31 days   6 28 days.

7 From the calendar above, find the months in which there are five Saturdays.

8 How do you know that the year shown above is not a leap year?

9 How many days are there in a leap year?

Parents' meetings are held on the second Wednesday in the 2nd, 5th, 9th and 11th months of the year.

10 From the calendar above, find the date of each meeting.

11 On which day does each of these birthdays fall?

Jane   8th Feb.   Stephen 30th Sept.
David 1st April   John   20th Oct.
Mary 28th Aug.   Susan   7th March

12 All the children named above are 9 years old. Write their names in order of age, the oldest first.

When reckoning periods of time in days, remember to count the last day but not the first day.

Who is the older and by how many days:

13 Stephen or John   14 Mary or Stephen

15 David or Susan   16 Jane or David?

17 Ann is 7 months older than David. In which month is her birthday?

Tony made this chart of the members of his family and their ages this year.

	Age
Grandmother	55
Grandfather	56
Mother	31
Father	33
Tony	9

How many years older is:
1 Grandfather than Tony
2 Grandmother than Mother?
3 How old will each member of the family be in the year 2000?

In which century is each of these years?
4 1892   5 1750   6 1924
7 2001   8 1596   9 1262

Write the following dates in shortened form, using figures only.
10 twenty-third of August, nineteen hundred and twenty
11 the third of June, eighteen ninety-two
12 the tenth of March, nineteen eighty-four

Write these dates in full, using words only.
13 1.1.79   14 11.11.84   15 12.8.85

16 James was born on 2.3.80. Write in figures the exact date on which he will be 30 years old.

Number the four rules, problems

A The heights of five children are given in the table.

	m	cm
Susan	1	36.5
Jane	1	52.5
Tim	1	43.5
John	1	34.5
Peter	1	18

1 Write the height of each child in cm.
2 Find the difference in height between the tallest and the shortest child.

Mr Brown is 1 m 82.5 cm tall.
How much taller is he than:

3 Susan   4 Tim   5 John?
6 Find the total height of the boys.
7 Divide this answer by 3 to find the average height of the boys.
8 Find the average height of the girls.
9 Find the total height of all the children.
10 Divide this answer by 5 to find the average height of all the children.

B Stair carpet can be bought for £9·78 per metre.

How much will these lengths of carpet cost?

1 9 m   2 18 m   3 5 m   4 15 m

5 Approximately how many metres can be bought for £100?
6 Susan had £36·15 in the bank.
She drew out £19·00 for a school journey.
How much had she left?

The table shows Tom's weekly savings.

Jan. 20	Jan. 27	Feb. 3	Feb. 10	Feb. 17
45p	75p	£1·25	£1·10	£0·95

7 Find his average weekly savings.
8 How much less than £10 has he saved?
9 Rachel spent £1·84 and found she had 98p left. How much had she at first?
10 Claire had £5. She bought 3 boxes of chocolates each costing 85p.
How much had she left?

C Here is the net mass shown on the label of some tins of food bought by mother.

Corned beef	Rice pudding	Potatoes
340 g	440 g	538 g

Find in kg the net mass of:

1 4 tins of corned beef
2 5 tins of rice pudding
3 6 tins of potatoes.
4 How much less than 7 kg is the total net mass?
5 6 metres of material is cut into 8 equal lengths. How long is each length?

The number of people attending a concert was as follows.
Mon. 196   Tues. 157   Wed. 139

6 Find the total attendance.
7 Find the average daily attendance.

There are 176 pages in Anna's reading book. She has read 38 pages.

8 How long will it take her to finish the book if she reads six pages each day?

D

Special Trip	Brigton-on-Sea	
	Adults	£6·36
	Children	half-price

Find the total cost of the fares for:

1 2 adults and 3 children
2 18 children and a teacher.
3 How much change is there from a £5 note after paying for one child?

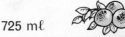

Squasho Orange drink	725 ml

4 When water is added, there is six times as much to drink. How many litres is that?

The number of children passing a life-saving test was:
class 1 24   class 2 28   class 3
class 4 27   class 5 18   class 6

5 Find the total number who passed.
6 What was the average number of passes per class?

Fractions

A Make sure you understand this diagram.

one whole one

By placing the edge of a ruler along the vertical lines in the diagram, you can compare the fractions shown.

Use the diagram to help you find these answers.

Which fraction is the larger?

1 $\frac{1}{4}$ or $\frac{1}{3}$ 2 $\frac{1}{10}$ or $\frac{1}{8}$ 3 $\frac{1}{5}$ or $\frac{1}{6}$

4 $\frac{3}{8}$ or $\frac{1}{4}$ 5 $\frac{2}{3}$ or $\frac{1}{2}$ 6 $\frac{3}{5}$ or $\frac{5}{6}$

Write each of the following, putting in the missing sign >, < or = in place of ●.

7 $\frac{2}{5} ● \frac{1}{4}$ 8 $\frac{2}{3} ● \frac{5}{6}$ 9 $\frac{1}{2} ● \frac{5}{10}$

10 $\frac{1}{3} ● \frac{3}{8}$ 11 $\frac{3}{10} ● \frac{1}{4}$ 12 $\frac{3}{4} ● \frac{4}{5}$

13 $\frac{4}{6} ● \frac{2}{3}$ 14 $\frac{4}{5} ● \frac{5}{8}$ 15 $\frac{9}{10} ● \frac{5}{6}$

Arrange these fractions in order of size, putting the largest first.

16 $\frac{1}{2}, \frac{2}{3}, \frac{4}{5}$ 17 $\frac{1}{3}, \frac{2}{5}, \frac{3}{8}$

18 $\frac{1}{8}, \frac{3}{10}, \frac{1}{6}$ 19 $\frac{2}{3}, \frac{5}{8}, \frac{3}{4}$

20 $\frac{4}{5}, \frac{7}{10}, \frac{3}{4}$ 21 $\frac{7}{8}, \frac{5}{6}, \frac{9}{10}$

Find the value of these fractions of 360.

22 $\frac{1}{2}, \frac{1}{4}, \frac{1}{5}, \frac{1}{6}, \frac{1}{8}, \frac{1}{9}, \frac{1}{10}$

Look again at the diagram at the top of the page.

What happens to the size of the parts of the same whole one when the fraction has a numerator of 1 and:

23 the denominator becomes larger

24 the denominator becomes smaller?

B Look at the diagram.

1 How many eighths are there in $\frac{3}{4}$?

2 Write: $\frac{3}{4} = \frac{\square}{8}$.

3 How many tenths are there in $\frac{1}{5}$?

4 Write: $\frac{1}{5} = \frac{\square}{10}$.

5 How many sixths are there in $\frac{1}{2}$?

6 Write: $\frac{1}{2} = \frac{\square}{6}$.

Write and complete the following.

7 $\frac{3}{5} = \frac{\square}{10}$ 8 $\frac{1}{3} = \frac{2}{\square}$ 9 $\frac{1}{2} = \frac{\square}{8}$

10 $\frac{2}{3} = \frac{\square}{6}$ 11 $\frac{1}{2} = \frac{5}{\square}$ 12 $\frac{4}{5} = \frac{\square}{10}$

> Look at each of the answers above. Notice that if the **numerator** and the **denominator** of a fraction are **multiplied** by the **same number**, the value of the fraction is unchanged.

Equivalent means 'equal in value to'.

13 Copy and complete the following sets of equivalent fractions.

$S = \{\frac{1}{2}, \frac{\square}{4}, \frac{\square}{6}, \frac{\square}{8}, \frac{\square}{10}, \frac{\square}{100}\}$

$T = \{\frac{1}{3}, \frac{\square}{6}, \frac{\square}{9}, \frac{\square}{12}, \frac{\square}{15}, \frac{\square}{18}\}$

$U = \{\frac{1}{4}, \frac{\square}{8}, \frac{\square}{16}, \frac{\square}{20}, \frac{\square}{24}, \frac{\square}{100}\}$

$V = \{\frac{1}{5}, \frac{\square}{10}, \frac{3}{\square}, \frac{\square}{20}, \frac{5}{\square}, \frac{\square}{100}\}$

$W = \{\frac{1}{10}, \frac{\square}{30}, \frac{4}{\square}, \frac{\square}{50}, \frac{9}{\square}, \frac{\square}{100}\}$

14 Copy and complete these sets of equivalent fractions.

$X = \{\frac{3}{4}, \frac{\square}{8}, \frac{12}{\square}, \frac{\square}{20}, \frac{18}{\square}, \frac{\square}{100}\}$

$Y = \{\frac{4}{5}, \frac{\square}{10}, \frac{20}{\square}, \frac{\square}{30}, \frac{40}{\square}, \frac{\square}{100}\}$

$Z = \{\frac{3}{10}, \frac{\square}{20}, \frac{15}{\square}, \frac{\square}{60}, \frac{21}{\square}, \frac{\square}{100}\}$

Write three fractions equivalent to:

15 $\frac{5}{6}$ 16 $\frac{5}{7}$ 17 $\frac{7}{9}$.

Write each of these fractions as twelfths. Then write them in order of size, the smallest first.

18 $\frac{1}{3}, \frac{1}{4}, \frac{1}{6}, \frac{1}{2}$ 19 $\frac{2}{3}, \frac{3}{4}, \frac{5}{6}, \frac{1}{2}$

Write each of these fractions as twentieths. Then write them in order of size, the largest first.

20 $\frac{1}{4}, \frac{3}{5}, \frac{1}{2}, \frac{1}{10}$ 21 $\frac{4}{5}, \frac{3}{4}, \frac{1}{2}, \frac{7}{10}$

Fractions

A

1. How many quarters are there in $\frac{2}{8}$?

2. Write: $\frac{2}{8} = \frac{\square}{4}$.

3. How many quarters are there in $\frac{6}{8}$?

4. Write: $\frac{6}{8} = \frac{\square}{4}$.

5. How many fifths are there in $\frac{8}{10}$?

6. Write: $\frac{8}{10} = \frac{\square}{5}$.

7. Write and complete the following sets of equivalent fractions.

$M = \{\frac{2}{6}, \frac{\square}{3}\}$ $N = \{\frac{5}{10}, \frac{\square}{2}\}$

$O = \{\frac{4}{10}, \frac{\square}{5}\}$ $P = \{\frac{3}{12}, \frac{\square}{4}\}$

$Q = \{\frac{9}{12}, \frac{\square}{4}\}$ $R = \{\frac{10}{20}, \frac{\square}{2}\}$

> Look at each of the answers above. Notice that if the **numerator** and the **denominator** of a fraction are **divided** by the **same number**, the value of the fraction is unchanged.

B

		whole	one		

1. Into how many equal parts is the whole one divided?

2. What fraction of the whole one is one of the equal parts?

3. What fraction of the whole one is shaded? Write: $\frac{2}{8} = \frac{2 \div 2}{8 \div 2} = \frac{1}{4}$.

4. What fraction of the whole one is unshaded? Write: $\frac{6}{8} = \frac{6 \div 2}{8 \div 2} = \frac{3}{4}$.

This process is called **cancelling** the fraction.

The working to questions **3** and **4** is usually set down like this.

$$\frac{\overset{1}{\cancel{2}}}{\underset{4}{\cancel{8}}} = \frac{1}{4} \qquad\qquad \frac{\overset{3}{\cancel{6}}}{\underset{4}{\cancel{8}}} = \frac{3}{4}$$

Cancel the following fractions by dividing the numerator and the denominator

by 2   5 $\frac{2}{14}$ 6 $\frac{2}{18}$ 7 $\frac{2}{50}$ 8 $\frac{2}{26}$

by 3.   9 $\frac{3}{9}$ 10 $\frac{3}{15}$ 11 $\frac{9}{21}$ 12 $\frac{15}{27}$

Cancel the following fractions.

13 $\frac{8}{10}$ 14 $\frac{9}{15}$ 15 $\frac{10}{12}$ 16 $\frac{6}{16}$

C

By cancelling, complete the following.

1. $\frac{8}{16} = \frac{\square}{8} = \frac{\square}{4} = \frac{\square}{2}$ 2. $\frac{8}{12} = \frac{\square}{6} = \frac{\square}{3}$

3. $\frac{12}{18} = \frac{\square}{9} = \frac{\square}{3}$ 4. $\frac{16}{20} = \frac{\square}{10} = \frac{\square}{5}$

A fraction which cannot be cancelled is said to be in its **lowest terms**.

Find which of the following fractions are in their lowest terms.

5. $\frac{7}{8}$ $\frac{9}{20}$ $\frac{5}{9}$ $\frac{7}{14}$ $\frac{8}{24}$ $\frac{5}{13}$

Cancel each of these fractions and write each in its lowest terms.

6 $\frac{4}{12}$ 7 $\frac{8}{12}$ 8 $\frac{8}{16}$ 9 $\frac{12}{16}$ 10 $\frac{4}{20}$

11 $\frac{10}{20}$ 12 $\frac{16}{20}$ 13 $\frac{25}{50}$ 14 $\frac{50}{100}$ 15 $\frac{75}{10}$

D

1. How many counters are there?

   How many are:

2. coloured   3 white?

   Write in its lowest terms the fraction of the counters which is:

4. coloured   5 white.

   Write the answer to each of the following in its lowest terms.

6. Jane had saved 30p. She bought a note book for 9p. What fraction of her money a did she spend   b was left?

7. A length of wood measures 50 cm. 15 cm is sawn off. What fraction of the length: a is sawn off   b remains?

A	C

8. Measure in mm the line AB.

9. What fraction of AB is   a AC   b CB

What fraction in its lowest terms is:

10 20p of £1   17 350 m of 1 km

11 75p of £1   18 50 g of $\frac{1}{2}$ kg

12 250 ml of 1 l   19 150 g of $\frac{1}{2}$ kg

13 700 ml of 1 l   20 15 s of 1 min

14 40 cm of 1 m   21 8 h of 1 day

15 60 cm of 1 m   22 45 min of 1 h

16 100 m of 1 km   23 3 months of 1 year

Fractions

A

The table shows the scores of four children in a Cycling Proficiency test. Each score was out of 100.

Roy	Stephen	Kate	Claire
85	75	70	90

1 Write in its lowest terms the fraction of the total points scored by each child.

In a sponsored walk, six children each tried to walk 30 kilometres.
The table shows how far each walked.

Richard	21 km	Rachel	27 km
Andrew	20 km	Carol	18 km
Michael	25 km	Joan	24 km

2 Write in its lowest terms the fraction of the 30 km walked by each child.

The table shows the amounts of money some children took on a school outing and the amount each spent.

	Mary	Jane	Susan
amount taken	£1·00	90p	£1·50
amount spent	65p	60p	90p

3 Write in its lowest terms the fraction of her money spent by each girl.

The rectangle contains 60 small squares.

4 Write in its lowest terms the fraction of the whole which is marked **W, X, Y, Z**.

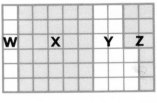

B

one whole one

1 What fraction of the whole one:
 a is the square shaded ■
 b are the squares shaded ☐?

2 What fraction of the whole one is the sum of the shaded squares?

Write: $\frac{1}{12} + \frac{7}{12} = \frac{\square}{12} = \frac{\square}{3}$.

In the same way, find the answers in their lowest terms to the following.

3 $\frac{1}{12} + \frac{5}{12}$ 4 $\frac{3}{8} + \frac{1}{8}$ 5 $\frac{2}{7} + \frac{3}{7}$

6 $\frac{1}{10} + \frac{7}{10}$ 7 $\frac{2}{10} + \frac{5}{10}$ 8 $\frac{7}{20} + \frac{9}{20}$

9 $\frac{29}{100} + \frac{21}{100}$ 10 $\frac{1}{15} + \frac{4}{15}$ 11 $\frac{2}{9} + \frac{4}{9}$

Write the answers in their lowest terms.

12 $\frac{3}{4} - \frac{1}{4}$ 13 $\frac{7}{8} - \frac{5}{8}$ 14 $\frac{7}{10} - \frac{3}{10}$

15 $\frac{7}{12} - \frac{4}{12}$ 16 $\frac{7}{9} - \frac{1}{9}$ 17 $\frac{5}{6} - \frac{1}{6}$

Write each of the following with a denominator of 100.

18 $\frac{1}{2}$ 19 $\frac{1}{4}$ 20 $\frac{1}{5}$ 21 $\frac{1}{20}$

22 $\frac{3}{4}$ 23 $\frac{3}{5}$ 24 $\frac{7}{10}$ 25 $\frac{2}{25}$

C

To add or subtract unlike fractions, change them first to fractions with the same denominator.

Examples	$\frac{1}{4} + \frac{3}{8}$ = $\frac{2}{8} + \frac{3}{8}$ = $\frac{5}{8}$
	$\frac{1}{2} - \frac{1}{3}$ = $\frac{3}{6} - \frac{2}{6}$ = $\frac{1}{6}$

Write the answers to the following in their lowest terms.

1 $\frac{3}{8} + \frac{1}{4}$ 2 $\frac{1}{6} + \frac{2}{3}$ 3 $\frac{3}{5} + \frac{1}{10}$

4 $\frac{1}{2} + \frac{3}{12}$ 5 $\frac{3}{4} + \frac{1}{8}$ 6 $\frac{1}{3} + \frac{5}{9}$

7 $\frac{1}{2} - \frac{1}{6}$ 8 $\frac{3}{4} - \frac{5}{8}$ 9 $\frac{5}{6} - \frac{1}{3}$

10 $\frac{7}{12} - \frac{1}{4}$ 11 $\frac{4}{5} - \frac{3}{10}$ 12 $\frac{3}{4} - \frac{2}{3}$

Write and complete, using the sign >, < or = in place of ●.

13 $\frac{3}{4}$ ● $\frac{5}{6}$ 14 $\frac{2}{3}$ ● $\frac{1}{2}$ 15 $\frac{1}{4}$ ● $\frac{6}{24}$

16 $\frac{75}{100}$ ● $\frac{7}{10}$ 17 $\frac{5}{8}$ ● $\frac{2}{3}$ 18 $\frac{5}{9}$ ● $\frac{3}{6}$

Change each of these fractions to fractions with the same denominator. Then write them in order of size, the largest first.

19 $\frac{1}{2}$ $\frac{5}{6}$ $\frac{3}{4}$ $\frac{7}{12}$

20 $\frac{1}{2}$ $\frac{1}{3}$ $\frac{2}{3}$ $\frac{5}{6}$

21 $\frac{1}{2}$ $\frac{5}{16}$ $\frac{3}{4}$ $\frac{7}{8}$

Fractions

A The table shows Jane's score in each of three tests.

	marks scored	possible marks
Maths	45	60
English	64	80
Science	12	20

1 Find, in its lowest terms, the fraction of the possible mark she scored in each test.

2 Ann spent 90p which was $\frac{5}{6}$ of her pocket-money. How much pocket-money does she receive?

3 Gail spent $\frac{1}{4}$ of her money on sweets and $\frac{1}{3}$ on gifts.
What fraction of her money had she left?

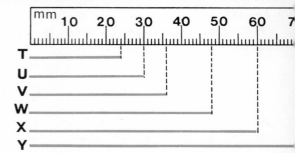

The line **Y** is 72 mm long.
What fraction, in its lowest terms, is the line:

4 **T** of **Y** 5 **U** of **Y** 6 **V** of **Y**
7 **W** of **Y** 8 **X** of **Y** 9 **T** of **V**?

10 9 metres of cloth was divided into 12 equal lengths.
What fraction of 1 metre was each length

B Dividing a number by 2 is the same as finding $\frac{1}{2}$ of it.
Find a half of:

1 96 2 154 3 482 4 630.

Dividing a number by 3 is the same as finding a third of it.
Find $\frac{1}{3}$ of:

5 51 6 504 7 297 8 558.

What fraction do you find when a number is divided by:

9 4 10 7 11 9 12 10?

Look at these examples.
$19 \div 2 = \frac{19}{2} = 9\frac{1}{2}$
$31 \div 3 = \frac{31}{3} = 10\frac{1}{3}$
Notice that the remainder is expressed as a fraction.

Write and complete:

13 $11 \div 2 = \frac{11}{2} = \square$ 14 $17 \div 3 = \frac{\square}{3} = \square$
15 $38 \div 7 = \frac{\square}{7} = \square$ 16 $57 \div 4 = \frac{\square}{\square} = \square$.

In the same way, work the following.

17 $27 \div 4$ 18 $39 \div 8$ 19 $58 \div 5$
20 $80 \div 7$ 21 $95 \div 6$ 22 $73 \div 10$
23 $104 \div 9$ 24 $68 \div 3$ 25 $107 \div 8$

C Look at the following examples.
$27 \div 6 = \frac{\overset{9}{\cancel{27}}}{\cancel{6}_{2}} = \frac{9}{2} = 4\frac{1}{2}$

$76 \div 12 = \frac{\overset{19}{\cancel{76}}}{\cancel{12}_{3}} = \frac{19}{3} = 6\frac{1}{3}$

Notice that the fraction has been cancelled and then the answer found.

Write and complete:

1 $36 \div 8 = \frac{36}{8} = \frac{\square}{2} = \square$
2 $60 \div 9 = \frac{\square}{9} = \frac{20}{\square} = \square$.

In the same way, work the following.

3 $58 \div 4$ 4 $69 \div 6$ 5 $102 \div 8$
6 $42 \div 9$ 7 $54 \div 12$ 8 $74 \div 18$
9 $44 \div 14$ 10 $125 \div 15$ 11 $166 \div 20$
12 $155 \div 25$ 13 $248 \div 18$ 14 $312 \div 16$

Now work the following in the same way and then write each answer to the neare whole one.

Remember, if the fraction is a half or more, count on to the next unit.
If the fraction is less than a half, forget

15 £353 ÷ 5 16 88p ÷ 3 17 967 km ÷
18 526 g ÷ 4 19 118 km ÷ 6 20 £97 ÷ 7
21 147 m ÷ 9 22 150 kg ÷ 8 23 982 m ÷ 4
24 68 m ÷ 12 25 £76 ÷ 14 26 967 km ÷

Circles radius and diameter

A

The circle is an important shape.

1 Give a reason why wheels are circular in shape.

2 Name four circular coins.

3 Make a list of six other things which are circular in shape.

4 Get several circular objects, e.g. tin lids, plates, etc., of different sizes.

5 Place them in turn on a large sheet of paper and use each to draw a circle.

6 Cut out two of the large circles.

The outside line or perimeter of a circle is called its **circumference**.

7 Fold one of your large circles into two equal parts.

8 What is the name of each part?

9 Now fold the circle into quarters.

10 What is the name given to a quarter of a circle?

11 Fold another of your large circles into two equal parts and draw a line along the crease.

12 Do this again in several places and mark each crease line.

13 If you have done this carefully, all the lines will cross at one point which is the **centre** of the circle.

14 Measure in millimetres each of these lines.

15 What do you find out about their lengths? Each of these lines is called a **diameter** of the circle.

B

To draw circles accurately you must learn to use a **pair of compasses**.

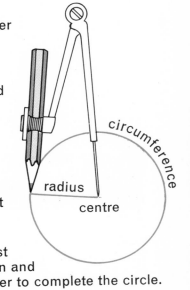

Make sure that the pencil holder is screwed up tightly.

Open the compasses and fix the point firmly in the paper.

Hold the compasses lightly with the thumb and first finger only.

Turn the compasses first in one direction and then in the other to complete the circle.

1 Draw a large circle. Mark its centre.

2 Draw a straight line from the centre to the circumference.
This line is called the **radius**.
Two or more are called **radii**.

3 What fraction of the diameter of a circle is the radius?

4 Draw six radii in the circle and then measure them in mm.

5 What do you discover about their lengths?

6 Now draw two more circles of different sizes.

7 Draw and measure six radii in each.

8 Are the radii in the same circle of equal length?

9 How many radii is it possible to draw in a circle?

10 How many diameters is it possible to draw in a circle?

11 How many lines of symmetry has a circle?

Discuss your answers with your teacher.

12 Practise using the compasses by drawing circles of different sizes.

Circles   shapes in circles

A

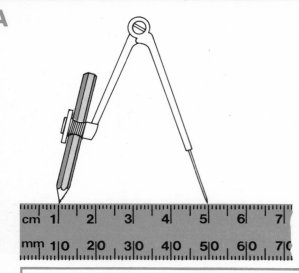

To draw a circle of given size, set the compasses to the length of the radius as shown in the diagram.

1 What is the radius shown on the ruler?

Draw circles of radius:

2 40 mm   3   35 mm   4   2.5 cm.

5 Find the length of the diameter of each circle. Check your answers by measuring

Draw circles, the diameters of which measure:

6 68 mm   7   56 mm   8   8.4 cm.

Using compasses and a set square, draw

9 a semicircle with a diameter of 40 mm

10 a quadrant with a radius of 60 mm.

Remember   All radii of the same circle are equal.
All diameters of the same circle are equal.
The diameter of a circle is twice the length of its radius.

B

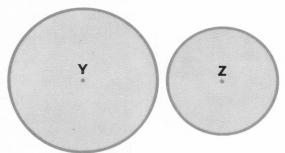

1 Measure the diameter of each circle **Y** and **Z**.

2 On a sheet of paper draw two circles the same size as **Y** and **Z**.

3 Cut out your circles and, by fitting them over **Y** and **Z**, test your accuracy.

4 Draw a circle of 25 mm radius.

5 Use a set square to draw two diameters which are perpendicular to one another.

6 Join the ends of the diameters at the circumference.

7 What is the shape you have made?

8 Test it with a ruler and set square.

C

1 Draw a circle of 30 mm radius.

2 With your compasses, mark off the radius round the circumference.

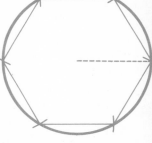

3 How many times can you do this?

4 Join the points on the circumference.

The shape you have made is called a **hexagon**.

5 How many sides has a hexagon?

6 Practise using your compasses by copying these patterns.

7 Now make up some patterns of your own.

Circles measuring diameter, circumference

A **Measuring the diameter**

To draw a circle of given size, the radius or the diameter must be known.

The diagram shows a method of measuring the diameter.

A TWO coin is used in the example.

1 Place a set square in line with a centimetre mark on a ruler.

2 Place the coin so that it touches the set square and the ruler.

3 Slide another set square along the edge of the ruler up to the edge of the coin.

4 Read its diameter from the scale.

In this way, find the diameter in mm of: 5 a penny 6 a FIVE 7 a TEN 8 £1.

9 Collect several tin lids of various sizes. Find in mm the diameter of each.

Using a metre ruler marked in cm, find to the nearest cm the diameter of the top and bottom of: 10 a bucket 11 a bowl.

B **Measuring the diameter**

The following method may be used to measure the diameter of a cylinder, e.g. a can.

1 Get a pair of calipers.

2 Open them and measure the diameter of the can.

3 Use a ruler to measure the distance between the arms of the calipers.

4 In the same way, find the diameters of other cans, bottles, etc.

C **Measuring the circumference**

1 To measure the rim of a bucket, plant pot, etc., wrap a tape-measure around the rim, holding the end firmly in place.

2 Read the measurement on the tape where it meets the other end.

3 A piece of string can be used instead of a tape. The length of string which fits exactly round the rim is then measured with a ruler.

D A circumference may be measured by rolling the object, e.g. a wheel.

1 Draw a straight line on the floor.

2 Make a chalk mark on the wheel and place it against a mark on the line.

3 Roll the wheel along the line until a complete turn has been made.

4 Mark on the line the end of the complete turn.

5 Measure the distance between the marks on the line. This is the length of the circumference.

6 Using the most suitable method, measure the circumference of jars, tyres, tins, etc.

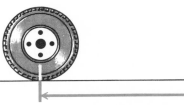

Making sure

A

Add 58 to each of the following.

1 89   **2** 160   **3** 145   **4** 996

Subtract 76 from each of the following.

5 152   **6** 400   **7** 311   **8** 1050

Multiply each of the following by 7.

9 86   **10** 49   **11** 97   **12** 135

Divide each of the following by 8.

13 416   **14** 608   **15** 912   **16** 1384

Cancel each of these fractions and write each in its lowest terms.

17 $\frac{6}{10}$ **18** $\frac{4}{20}$ **19** $\frac{75}{100}$ **20** $\frac{8}{12}$

21 $\frac{12}{16}$ **22** $\frac{35}{100}$ **23** $\frac{30}{48}$ **24** $\frac{80}{100}$

Write each of the following as a fraction. Then cancel and find the answer.

25 $145 \div 15$ **26** $324 \div 16$ **27** $475 \div 25$

28 $624 \div 18$ **29** $272 \div 14$ **30** $282 \div 12$

B

What number does one small division represent on each of the scales below?

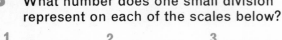

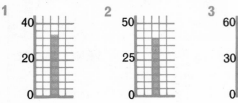

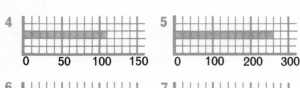

8 Find the number represented by each of the lines in **B1** to **7**.

Find the missing cost, price charged or quantity purchased.

	quantity purchased	price charged	cost
9	1.5 kg	£1·50 per kg	£□
10	□ g	60p per $\frac{1}{2}$ kg	30p
11	2 ℓ	□p per ℓ	90p
12	$\frac{3}{4}$ m	80p per m	□p
13	□ kg	£1·00 per 200 g	£5·00
14	5 m	□p per m	£2·00
15	500 mℓ	70p per ℓ	□p
16	□ g	£1·60 per kg	40p
17	3 ℓ	□p per ℓ	£2·10
18	0.1 kg	£2 per kg	□p
19	□ cm	£4 per m	£2
20	50 ℓ	£□ per ℓ	£100

C

Write the answers only.

1 Find the difference in value between the 4 in 84 and the 4 in 96.4.

2 Find the total value of: 3 FIFTIES, 3 TWENTIES, and 4 FIVES.

3 Out of 20 answers, James had 3 times as many right as he had wrong. How many did he have right?

4 Find the product of 7, 8 and 9.

5 The perimeter of a square is 18 cm. Find in mm the length of each side.

6 Using the least number, name the notes and coins used to pay a bill for £7·69.

7 A wheel has a circumference of 2.1 m. How far will it travel in 10 turns?

8 A medicine bottle holds 150 mℓ. How many doses of medicine each of 5 mℓ can be taken from the bottle?

How many grams are there in:

9 0.545 kg   **10** 1.65 kg   **11** 3.8 kg?

12 Find the number which is 8 more than three-quarters of 36.

Multiply each of the following by 10.

13 3.7   **14** 305   **15** 9.5 m   **16** £0·58

17 Which two prime numbers have a sum of 24 and a product of 95?

18 Find the total of 4 thousands, 9 hundreds, 2 tens and 56 tenths.

19 Find the sum of: 87p, 24p, 57p, £1·06.

Right angles

A

1 Cut out two strips from thin cardboard.

2 Place one on top of the other and fasten them with a paper fastener.
Meccano strips fastened with a nut and bolt may be used.

The two strips are the 'arms' of the angles you are about to make.

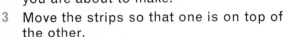

3 Move the strips so that one is on top of the other.

Turn the top strip only through:

4 1 right angle   5 3 right angles.

6 Now use a set square and draw lines to show the position of the strips in questions **4** and **5**.

Notice that the lines you have drawn are perpendicular to each other.

Describe the position of the strips when the top strip is turned through:

7 2 right angles   8 4 right angles.

What fraction of a complete turn is made when the top strip is turned through:

9 1 right angle   10 2 right angles

11 3 right angles?

**Remember
A right angle is a measure of an amount of turning.**

The hour-hand on this clock is pointing to 12.

To which number on the clock will it point when it has turned through:

12 1 right angle   13 2 right angles

14 3 right angles   15 4 right angles?

B

The picture shows Peter standing facing the blackboard.

He makes a **right** turn.

He has turned through a right angle.

Through how many right angles has he turned if:

1 he faces in the opposite direction

2 he turns completely around once?

Susan stands at O, facing north.
Turning **left**, through how many right angles does she turn to face:

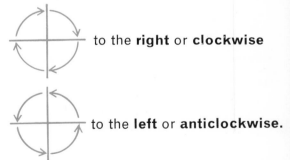

3 west   4 south

5 east?

John faces west.
Turning **right**, through how many right angles does he turn to face:

6 north   7 south   8 east?

Turnings can be made:

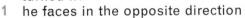

to the **right** or **clockwise**

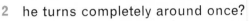

to the **left** or **anticlockwise**.

David stands facing east.

To face north, through how many right angles does he turn:

9 clockwise   10 anticlockwise?

Mary stands facing south.

In which direction is she facing if she turns:

11 clockwise through 3 right angles

12 anticlockwise through 3 right angles?

Angles the compass

A Many centuries ago, the people of Babylon divided a complete turn into 360 degrees (360°).

This same unit of measurement is still used today for measuring **turns** or **rotations**.

1 How many degrees are there in a right angle?

Write the following table, filling in the missing numbers.

2 $\frac{1}{4}$ of a complete turn = ☐ right angle = ☐ degrees

3 $\frac{1}{2}$ of a complete turn = ☐ right angles = ☐ degrees

4 $\frac{3}{4}$ of a complete turn = ☐ right angles = ☐ degrees

5 1 complete turn = ☐ right angles = ☐ degrees

6 How many degrees are there at the centre of a circle?

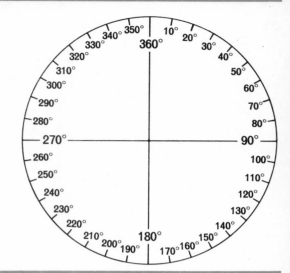

B

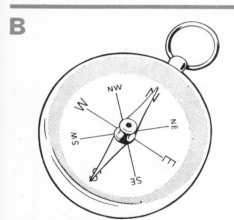

Get a compass. It is an instrument used to find direction. Read about it in an encyclopaedia.

Examine the compass and find out how it is made.

Find out how to make a simple compass.

1 Place the compass on a flat surface and watch the needle. When it comes to rest it points **north (N)**.

2 Use the compass to find north in your class-room.

Stand facing north and then by making turns of 90° face

3 east　4 south　5 west.

Take the compass into the playground and repeat the same exercise.

C The compass card shows eight points of a compass.

You can make one of your own.

1 a On a piece of stiff paper, draw and cut out a circle of 5 cm radius.

b By folding through the centre, divide the circle into 8 equal parts.

c Mark the 8 points as shown in the diagram.

d How many degrees are there in each angle at the centre?

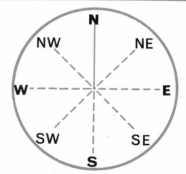

2 a Place the compass card on your desk and set it so that the north line points in the correct direction.

b Use a compass to do this.

c Stand up and then face in each of the 8 directions, turning clockwise.

Through how many degrees do you turn when turning clockwise from:

3 W to NW　4 SE to S　5 NE to S

6 SW to NW　7 NW to E　8 E to SW

9 N to NW　10 W to SE?

Angles   set squares

A   To draw and measure angles of 90° and 45°

Use stiff paper to make angle cards.

1   Draw and cut out a semicircle with a radius of 6 cm.

fold and cut

fold and cut

2   By folding, divide the semicircle into two equal parts. Mark the fold and cut along it.

3   In a semicircle   **a** how many right angles   **b** how many degrees are there?

4   Take one right angle and fold it to make two equal angles, each of which is a half right angle.

5   How many degrees are there in a half right angle?

6   Cut out an angle of 45° and mark its size.

To draw and measure angles of 60° and 30°

7   Draw a circle of 6 cm radius and mark off the radius round the circumference. (see page 60, Section **C**)

8   Join the points through the centre.

9   How many equal angles are there?

10   How many degrees in each?

11   Cut out two of the angles.

12   On one, mark the number of degrees.

13   Fold and cut the other in half to make an angle of 30°. Mark its size.

Angles **less than 1 right angle** (90°) are called **acute angles**. Draw five acute angles.

B

1   Get a pair of set squares like those shown in the drawing. Each is a triangle of a different shape.

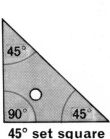
45° set square

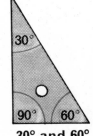
30° and 60° set square

2   Place each set square on a piece of paper. Draw round each of them.

3   Test each angle in your drawings with your angle cards and mark each angle on your drawing as shown.

Use your angle cards or a pair of set squares to measure in degrees these angles.

4

5

6

By fitting your angle cards or the set square angles together, draw the following.

7   8

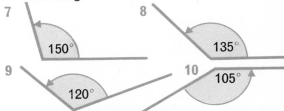
150°   135°

9   10
120°   105°

11   Now draw the angles again making the arms   **a** shorter   **b** longer.

Notice that the size of the angles is not changed.

Angles **greater than a right angle** but **less than 2 right angles** are called **obtuse angles**. Draw five obtuse angles.

Measures   length, mass, capacity

A
Write and complete:
1 1 cm = ☐ mm   2 1 m = ☐ cm
3 0.1 cm = ☐ mm   4 0.1 m = ☐ cm
5 0.5 cm = ☐ mm   6 0.5 m = ☐ cm.

Write and complete:
7 156 cm = ☐ m ☐ cm = ☐ m
8 980 cm = ☐ m ☐ cm = ☐ m
9 1257 cm = ☐ m ☐ cm = ☐ m
10 1085 cm = ☐ m ☐ cm = ☐ m
11 2050 cm = ☐ m ☐ cm = ☐ m.

Write in cm.
12 6.83 m   13 2.8 m   14 5.75 m
15 0.75 m   16 8.62 m   17 10.40 m

Write and complete:
18 1 km = ☐ m   19 $\frac{1}{2}$ km = ☐ m
20 $\frac{1}{4}$ km = ☐ m   21 $\frac{3}{4}$ km = ☐ m
22 0.1 km = ☐ m   23 0.6 km = ☐ m.

Write and complete:
24 3800 mm = ☐ m ☐ mm = ☐ m
25 6750 mm = ☐ m ☐ mm = ☐ m
26 2195 mm = ☐ m ☐ mm = ☐ m
27 2400 m = ☐ km ☐ m = ☐ km
28 3500 m = ☐ km ☐ m = ☐ km.

Write in m.
29 5.8 km   30 3.7 km   31 0.3 km
32 1.9 km   33 4.2 km   34 2.6 km

B
Write to the nearest metre.
1 450 cm   2 389 cm   3 536 cm
4 294 cm   5 720 cm   6 810 cm
7 4.13 m   8 3.45 m   9 6.7 m

Write to the nearest $\frac{1}{2}$ metre.
10 349 cm   11 217 cm   12 580 cm
13 220 cm   14 4.85 m   15 3.25 m

Write to the nearest metre.
16 5700 mm   17 2650 mm   18 4450 mm
19 8390 mm   20 6920 mm   21 3466 mm
22 4750 mm   23 2183 mm   24 9500 mm

Write to the nearest $\frac{1}{2}$ metre.
25 3150 mm   26 1550 mm   27 4800 mm
28 5400 mm   29 2300 mm   30 7190 mm

C

1 Measure in mm WX, XY and YZ.   2 Find their total length.
3 Find the difference in mm between the total length and a straight line from W to Z.

D
Write and complete:
1 1 kg = ☐ g   2 $\frac{1}{2}$ kg = ☐ g
3 $\frac{1}{4}$ kg = ☐ g   4 $\frac{3}{4}$ kg = ☐ g
5 0.1 kg = ☐ g   6 0.5 kg = ☐ g
7 2.4 kg = ☐ g   8 3.3 kg = ☐ g
9 4500 g = ☐ kg ☐ g = ☐ kg
10 1450 g = ☐ kg ☐ g = ☐ kg
11 6875 g = ☐ kg ☐ g = ☐ kg.

How many mℓ in:
12 1 ℓ   13 $\frac{1}{2}$ ℓ   14 $\frac{1}{4}$ ℓ   15 $\frac{3}{4}$ ℓ
16 0.5 ℓ 17 0.3 ℓ 18 0.7 ℓ 19 0.9 ℓ?

Write to the nearest kg.
20 4900 g   21 3440 g   22 6750 g
23 2610 g   24 5160 g   25 3455 g
26 4.670 kg   27 3.480 kg   28 7.910 kg

Write to the nearest $\frac{1}{2}$ kg.
29 1440 g   30 2650 g   31 4700 g
32 3200 g   33 3300 g   34 5080 g
35 8.160 kg   36 9.400 kg   37 7.590 kg

What decimal fraction of 1 litre is:
38 100 mℓ   39 400 mℓ   40 600 mℓ
41 800 mℓ   42 200 mℓ   43 300 mℓ?

Puzzle corner

A

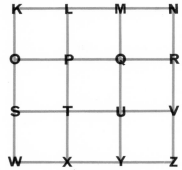

This is the plan of a flower-bed which has been laid out in squares, with a narrow path round each square. The side of each small square measures 5 metres.

A path from point **W** to point **L** can be taken in many ways. Here are two of them. **W** to **X** to **T** to **P** to **L**
W to **S** to **O** to **K** to **L**

Draw the diagram and show in different colours three paths of equal length

1 from **W** to **R**   2 from **N** to **X**.

Write in metres the shortest distance by the paths

3 from **Z** to **L**   4 from **K** to **V**.

5 Find the total length of all the paths.

C

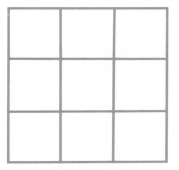

In the diagram there are many different squares.

1 Look at it carefully and find how many squares there are altogether.

In a code each letter is given a number. The following are some of the letters with their numbers.

V=10	W=5	X=3	Y=7	Z=4

Write in figures the answers to the following, which are written in code.

2 Add V, W and X and take away Z.

3 Divide the product of V and X by W.

4 $2Y-(X+Z)$ 5 $\dfrac{Y \times Z}{V}$ 6 $\dfrac{6V}{W}$

B

David is five years old and his brother Peter is 9.

1 How much older will Peter be than David in three years' time?

2 How old was Peter when he was twice as old as David?

3 How old was Peter when he was three times David's age?

Look at the number series and in each case write the two numbers which you think should come next.

4	1	2	4	8	16	☐	☐
5	1	3	6	10	15	☐	☐
6	54	48	42	36	30	☐	☐
7	8	4	2	1	$\frac{1}{2}$	☐	☐
8	4	2	8	4	16	☐	☐
9	19.2	9.6	4.8	2.4	1.2	☐	☐

D

1 If the letters of the alphabet are numbered so that A is 1, B is 2 and C is 3 and so on, what word do these numbers represent?

13	1	9	4	5	14

Pythagoras, a famous Greek mathematician, was very interested in numbers. He made many discoveries about them. The following is one of them.

The sum of the consecutive **odd** numbers, starting with 1, is always a square number, e.g. $1+3 = 4 = 2^2$ $1+3+5 = 9 = 3^2$.

2 Find the odd numbers which when added together make 10^2.

3 From a book in the library, read about Pythagoras and the discoveries he made. You will meet his name later.

Decimal fractions   tenths and hundredths

A

X Y	
4 4 3 . 3	

1 How many times is the value of the 4 marked X greater than the 4 marked Y?

X Y	
4 4 3 . 3	

2 How many times is the value of the 3 marked X greater than the 3 marked Y?

M N	
8 8 5 . 5	

3 How many times is the value of the 8 marked N less than the 8 marked M?

M N	
8 8 5 . 5	

4 How many times is the value of the 5 marked N less than the 5 marked M?

By moving each figure **one place to the left** multiply the following by 10.

5 0.4   6 8.6   7 17.3
8 10.5   9 116.1   10 203.4
11 3.6 cm 12 9.2 cm 13 £1·50

By moving each figure **one place to the right** divide the following by 10.

14 2   15 74   16 89
17 106   18 223   19 1107
20 52 cm 21 11 cm 22 £19·00

B

You have learned that when a figure is moved **one place to the right**

Th	H	T	U	t	
1	1	1	1	1	1

The 1 decreases 10 times for each place.

it is **one tenth** of its former value.

In this diagram, the figure 1 in the tenths column is moved **one place to the right**.

Its value therefore is 10 times **smaller** than one tenth $\frac{1}{10}$.

You must now find the value of **one tenth of one tenth**   or $\frac{1}{10}$ of $\frac{1}{10}$.

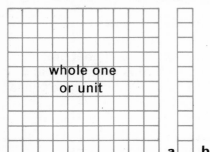

Look at the diagram.

1 How many strips like **a** are there in the whole one?
2 What fraction of the whole one is strip **a**?

3 How many small squares like **b** are there in strip **a**?
4 What fraction of strip **a** is a small square?

5 How many small squares are there in the whole one?
6 What fraction of the whole one is one small square?

Copy and complete:

	U	tenths	hundredths
7 one strip is $\frac{1}{\square}$ of the whole one ⟶	0	1	
8 one small square is $\frac{1}{10}$ of $\frac{1}{10}$ or $\frac{1}{\square}$ of the whole one. ⟶	0	0	1

Write as decimal fractions.
9 3 hundredths   10 5 hundredths   11 9 hundredths

> The figure in the **first place** after the decimal point is **tenths**.
> The figure in the **second place** after the decimal point is **hundredths**.

Decimal fractions tenths and hundredths

A

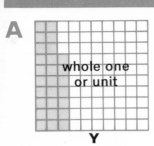 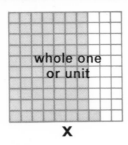

Y   X

How many hundredths of the whole one **Y** are:

1 shaded   2 unshaded?

How many hundredths of the whole one **X** are:

3 shaded   4 unshaded?

5 Write each answer as a decimal fraction.

On squared paper, draw diagrams to show by shading:

6 0.33   7 0.61   8 0.07   9 1.89.

10 Write under each diagram the decimal fraction which is unshaded.

Write the following as decimals.

11 79 hundredths   12 153 hundredths

13 572 hundredths   14 308 hundredths

15 $13\frac{9}{100}$ 16 $70\frac{6}{100}$ 17 $30\frac{46}{100}$

B

What is the value of each figure underlined in these numbers?

1 50<u>3</u>.76   2 20.<u>8</u>4   3 <u>3</u>06.92

$$0.93 = \frac{9}{10} + \frac{3}{100} = \frac{93}{100}$$

Write in the same way:

4 0.27   5 3.46   6 2.08.

Copy and complete the following.

7 7.63 = ☐ units ☐ tenths ☐ hundredths

8 7.63 = ☐ tenths ☐ hundredths

9 9.04 = ☐ tenths ☐ hundredths

10 9.04 = ☐ hundredths

11 6.9 = ☐ tenths

12 6.9 = ☐ hundredths

13 14.56 = ☐ tenths ☐ hundredths

14 14.56 = ☐ hundredths

C

1 How many times is the 2 marked Y greater than the 2 marked Z?

Y	Z
2 3 . 2	

2 How many times is the 7 marked Z less than the 7 marked Y?

Y	Z
3 7 . 4 7	

By moving each figure **two places to the left**, multiply the following by 100.

3 6.39   4 0.87   5 0.04

6 56.08   7 10.36   8 1.93

9 24.0   10 0.5   11 11.8

By moving each figure **two places to the right**, divide the following by 100.

12 374   13 250   14 3090

15 45   16 61   17 10

18 1224   19 7652   20 8

Write the answers only.

21 0.79×10 22 0.79×100

23 0.02×10 24 0.02×100

25 $56 \div 10$ 26 $56 \div 100$

27 $105 \div 10$ 28 $105 \div 100$

D

Write the answers only.

1 84.7×10 8 $908 \div 100$

2 7.83×10 9 $240 \div 100$

3 0.64×100 10 £12·00 ÷ 100

4 0.58×100 11 $\frac{873}{10}$

5 0.76×100 12 $\frac{906}{100}$

6 £0·02 × 100   13 $£\frac{104}{100}$

7 £0·07 × 100   14 $£\frac{425}{100}$

Write the numbers below in order of size, the smallest first.

15	7	70	0.7	7.07
16	2.8	28	2.83	28.6
17	0.58	0.6	0.5	0.63
18	0.4	0.41	0.39	0.47
19	0.8	0.79	1.0	0.11
20	0.53	0.2	2.0	1.49

Decimal fractions tenths and hundredths

A

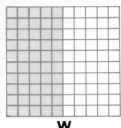 **W**   **X**   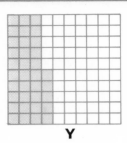 **Y**   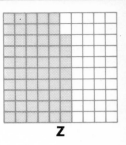 **Z**

1   In each of the whole ones **W**, **X**, **Y** and **Z**, how many hundredths are shaded?

Write as decimal fractions the part of each whole one which is   2   shaded   3   unshaded.

Write as a vulgar fraction in its lowest terms the part of each whole one which is

                                            4   shaded   5   unshaded.

B   Copy and complete the following using > , < or = in place of ● .

1   0.1   ●   0.01
2   0.05   ●   0.2
3   0.50   ●   0.5
4   0.09   ●   0.3
5   0.10   ●   0.1
6   0.3   ●   0.06

7   0.36   ● $\frac{36}{100}$
8   0.45   ● $\frac{1}{2}$
9   $\frac{5}{10}$ ●   0.53
10   0.11   ● $\frac{9}{100}$
11   0.77   ● $\frac{3}{4}$
12   0.82   ● $\frac{79}{100}$

Write the value of each of the figures underlined.

13   306.4<u>6</u>   14   215.0<u>7</u>   15   182.7<u>9</u>
16   <u>1</u>9.67   17   10.0<u>8</u>   18   <u>2</u>03.15

Change each of the following to a vulgar fraction in its lowest terms.

19   0.4   20   0.8   21   0.04
22   0.5   23   0.05   24   0.26
25   0.15   26   0.48   27   0.39

Change each of the following to hundredths and then write each as a decimal fraction.

28   $\frac{1}{20}$ 29 $\frac{7}{20}$ 30 $\frac{19}{20}$
31   $\frac{1}{50}$ 32 $\frac{3}{50}$ 33 $\frac{23}{50}$
34   $\frac{1}{25}$ 35 $\frac{7}{25}$ 36 $\frac{19}{25}$

C   In Britain a decimal currency is used. Up to now, you have been writing sums of money using a **pennies point** to separate the £s from the pence.

You must now think of the pennies point as a **decimal point**.

      1 TEN   = $\frac{1}{10}$ of £1   =   £0·1   or   £0·10
      1 penny   = $\frac{1}{100}$ of £1   =   £0·01

Look at the diagram.

Hundreds H	Tens T	Units U	tenths t	hundredths h
Hundreds of £s	Tens of £s	Units of £s	tenths of £s	hundredths of £s
£3	5	8	7	6

1   Write the value in money of each figure.

Write the value in money of each figure underlined.

2   £2<u>3</u>·64   3   £9·8<u>5</u>   4   £19·<u>4</u>0   5   £6<u>2</u>·09
6   £0·9<u>2</u>   7   £<u>3</u>03·50   8   £51·<u>7</u>5   9   £0·0<u>9</u>

Most other countries use a decimal currency which is based on a unit and 100 smaller units. For example, in France   1 franc = 100 centimes.

10   Write the names of six other countries which have a decimal currency. Find and write the names of the units used in each country.

Circles arcs

A

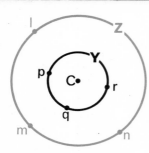

The two circles shown have the same centre, C.

Circles having the same centres are called **concentric** circles.

1 Measure in mm the radius of each of the circles **Y** and **Z**.

2 Write in mm the distance from the centre to each of the points l, m and n on circle **Z**.

3 Write in mm the distance from the centre to each of the points p, q and r on circle **Y**.

4 What do you discover?

5 Give the reason for this.

> **Remember**
> **All points on the circumference are of equal distance from its centre.**

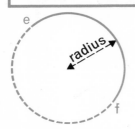

Any part of the circumference of a circle is called an **arc**.

In this diagram, ef is an arc of the circle.

Look at the circle **Z** above.
mn is an arc of the circle.

Write the letters which name:

6 two other arcs of circle **Z**

7 three arcs of circle **Y** above.

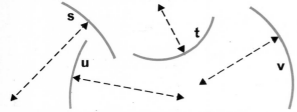

The diagrams show four different arcs.

8 Measure in mm the radius of each arc.

9 Which two arcs have the same radius?

B

1 Draw a line 40 mm long and mark it **AB**.

2 Set the compasses to a radius of 30 mm.

3 Using **A** as the centre, draw an arc.

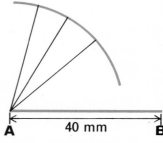

4 Draw lines from **A** to meet the arc.

5 What is the length of each line in mm?

6 Give the reason for this.

7 Draw another line 40 mm long and mark it **AB**.

8 Set the compasses to a radius of 35 mm.

9 Using **B** as the centre, draw an arc.

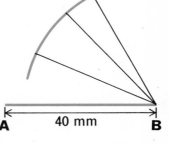

10 Draw lines from **B** to meet the arc and find the length of each in mm.

11 Why are all the lines the same length?

By drawing arcs of the same radius as in the two diagrams above, a shape can be made.

12 What is the name of the shape?

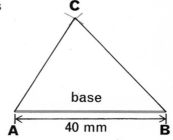

13 What is the length of each of its sides?

14 By drawing arcs, copy the triangle.

15 Draw the triangle again in the same way, but this time draw the sides **AC** and **BC** below the line **AB**.

16 In the same way, draw another shape with base of 60 mm and the other sides 50 mm and 45 mm.

Triangles and their sides

A A triangle is a shape which has three sides and three angles.
A triangle is usually named by letters.

The first is named by the letters **LMN**.

1 Name the other triangles in the same way.

2 Draw five triangles each of different shape and size using a ruler only.

3 Name each triangle with letters.

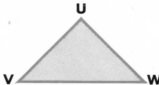

Drawing triangles with sides of given lengths

The lines **AB**, **AC** and **BC** show the lengths of the sides of triangle **ABC**.

4 Measure the length of each side in mm.

5 Draw **AB** which is the base of the triangle.

6 With centre **A** and a radius equal to **AC**, draw an arc.

7 With centre **B** and a radius equal to **BC**, draw an arc.

8 Draw lines from **A** and **B** to the point **C** where the arcs cut each other (intersect).

9 Letter the triangle you have drawn **ABC**.

10 On a sheet of paper, draw a triangle with the sides equal to the sides of the triangle **ABC**, but make the side **AC** the base.

11 Draw a triangle with the sides equal to the sides of triangle **ABC**, but make **BC** the base.

12 Cut out the three triangles you have drawn and fit one on top of the other.

13 What do you find about their size and shape?

B

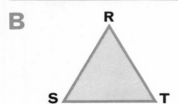

1 Measure in mm the sides of the triangle **RST**.

2 You should find the sides are of equal length.

Triangles with equal sides are called **equilateral triangles**. ('equilateral' means equal sides)

Draw equilateral triangles with sides:

3 65 mm   4 50 mm.

C

1 Measure in mm the sides of the triangle **UVW**.

2 You should find two sides are of equal length.

Triangles with two equal sides are called **isosceles triangles**. ('isosceles' means equal legs)

Draw an isosceles triangle with sides:

3 45 mm, 85 mm, 85 mm.

D

1 Measure in mm the sides of the triangle **XYZ**.

2 You should find the sides are of different lengths.

Triangles with sides of different lengths are called **scalene triangles**. ('scalene' means uneven)

Draw a scalene triangle with sides:

3 75 mm, 45 mm, 100 mm.

Triangles naming by angles

You have learned that different kinds of triangles are named according to the lengths of their sides.

Triangles are also named according to their angles.

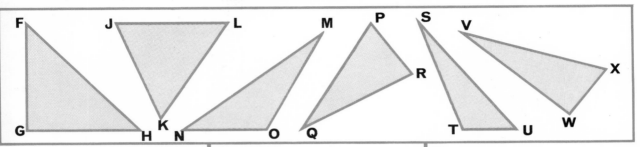

A

1 Use a set square and find in which of the triangles there is one right angle.

These triangles are called **right-angled triangles**.

2 Use a ruler and a set square to draw three right-angled triangles.

B

1 In which of the triangles are there three acute angles? An acute angle is less than 90°.

These triangles are called **acute-angled triangles**.

2 Using a ruler only, draw three acute-angled triangles.

C

1 In which of the triangles is there an obtuse angle? An obtuse angle is greater than 90°, but less than 180°.

These triangles are called **obtuse-angled triangles**.

2 Using a ruler only, draw three obtuse-angled triangles.

D Finding the sum of the angles in a triangle

1 a On gummed paper draw and cut out a large acute-angled triangle. Number the angles.
  b Tear off each angle and fit them together as shown in the diagram.
  c Stick them on to a piece of paper.

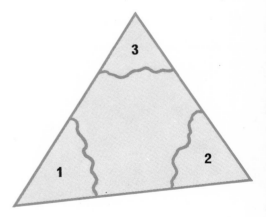

2 The three angles together make a straight angle. How many:
  a right angles
  b degrees are there in a straight angle?

3 Draw more triangles, right-angled, acute-angled and obtuse-angled. Repeat the exercise above and see if you get the same result each time.

4 Write and complete:
The three angles of a triangle together equal
  ☐ right angles   or   ☐ degrees.

5 Why is it impossible to draw a triangle in which there are:
  a 2 right angles   b 2 obtuse angles?

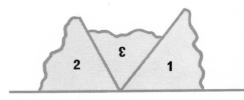

Triangles sides and angles

A

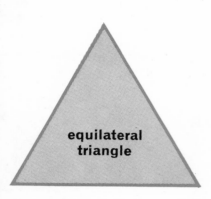

equilateral triangle

1 Draw and cut out an equilateral triangle with sides 90 mm long.

2 Get a 60° set square and fit it into each angle.

3 What is the size of each angle in an equilateral triangle?

4 Draw three more large equilateral triangles. Choose your own measurements for the sides. Use the 60° set square to find the size of the angles in each triangle.

5 Write what you have discovered about the angles of **equilateral** triangles.

B

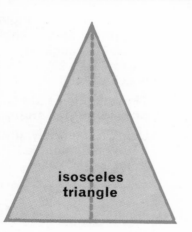

isosceles triangle

1 Draw and cut out an isoceles triangle with a base of 45 mm and two equal sides each of 80 mm.

2 Fold the triangle into two equal parts.

3 What do you discover about the angles at the base of the triangle?

4 Draw and cut out three more large isosceles triangles. Choose your own measurements for the sides.

5 Fold each triangle into two equal parts. Do the angles at the base fit?

6 Write what you have discovered about the angles opposite the two equal sides of an **isosceles** triangle.

C

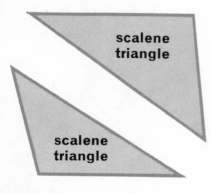

scalene triangle

scalene triangle

1 Measure in mm the sides of each of these scalene triangles.

2 Draw them on a sheet of paper, making each side double the length shown in the diagrams.

3 Cut out one triangle. Tear off each angle and place them on top of one another.

4 Cut out the other triangle and place the three angles together in the same way.

5 Write what you have discovered about the size of the angles of a **scalene** triangle.

D

You have cut out:
an equilateral triangle, isosceles triangles and scalene triangles.

Find, by folding, the number of lines of symmetry in:

1 an equilateral triangle   2 an isosceles triangle   3 a scalene triangle.

Sets

A

1 Use a capital letter and list in brackets the members of the following sets. Remember to separate the members with a comma.

D = {days of the week beginning with S}
R = {months of the year with 30 days}
E = {even numbers between 1 and 9}
O = {odd numbers between 6 and 18}
F = {factors of 16}

2 Describe each of these sets in words. The first is done for you.

C = {red, blue, yellow, green}
C = {four colours}

M = {January, February, March}
A = {lion, leopard, tiger, hyena}
T = { ▷ , ◥ , △ , ◣ }
U = {mm, cm, m, km}
N = {5, 10, 15, 20, 25}
K = {18, 15, 12, 9, 21, 6}

B

In each of the following sets, there is one member which does not belong. Write or draw it.

1 V = {car, truck, bus, bicycle}
2 C = { ○ , ◯ , ○ , ⬭ , ○ }
3 S = { ☐ , ☐ , ▭ , ☐ , ☐ }
4 T = {10, 50, 130, 25, 140}
5 N = {35, 70, 20, 53, 65}
6 Z = {21, 35, 27, 70, 49}

Some sets may have only one member or just a few members. Write the members of each of these sets.

7 X = {prime numbers between 20 and 28}
8 F = {factors of 15 other than 1 and 15}
9 O = {odd numbers between 94 and 100}
10 Write two sets of your own, each of which has one member only.
11 Write two sets of your own, one of which has two members and the other three members.

C

There is a short way of writing sets with many members. Look at this example.
M = {multiples of 5 less than 61}
M = {5, 10, 15, ... 50, 55, 60}
The three dots stand for 20, 25, 30, 35, 40, 45.

What do the dots stand for in each of these sets?
1 H = {Jan., Feb., March, ... Nov., Dec.}
2 R = {I, II, III, ... X, XI, XII}
3 Z = {9, 18, 27, ... 72, 81, 90}

In the same way, using dots, write the members of these sets.
4 T = {24-hour clock times shown hourly}
5 Q = {numbers less than 199 ending in 0}
6 F = {lengths in whole cm less than 1 m}
7 In the same way, using dots, write three sets of your own, each with many members.

D

In some sets the list of members goes on and on for ever. They have an infinite (unlimited) number of members.

Look at this example.
W = {whole numbers}
W = {1, 2, 3, 4, 5, ...}
1 Write the next five members of set W.

Write the next four members of each of these sets.
2 S = {multiples of 7}
S = {7, 14, 21, 28, ...}
3 F = {multiples of 50}
F = {50, 100, 150, 200, ...}

Using dots, write the members of these sets.
4 Q = {multiples of 8}
5 T = {whole numbers ending in 3}
6 D = {numbers divisible by 6}
7 Z = {multiples of 4 ending in 0}

Sets

A

Some sets have no members.
These sets are called **empty sets.**

Look at the example below.
The children in class 2 are put into
reading sets as shown.

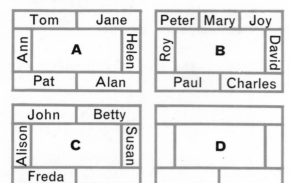

1 Write in brackets the members of these
sets. Name each set by a capital letter.
A ={the best readers}
B ={the good readers}
C ={the slow readers}
D ={the children who cannot read}

Set D has no members. It is an empty
set which is written { }.
Another way of writing an empty set is
by using the symbol ∅.
D =∅   or   D={ }

2 Some of the following are empty sets.
Pick them out and write them in two
ways. The first is done for you.
N ={circles with three sides}
N ={ }   or   N=∅
S ={teachers less than 1 m tall}
T ={triangles with four sides}
W={weeks with 8 days}
M ={fractions less than $\frac{1}{100}$}
G ={girls with short hair}
E ={cubes with 7 faces}
F ={fractions greater than $\frac{9}{10}$}

3 Describe three empty sets of your own
and write them as empty sets, as in
set N above.

B

In each of the following sets there is a
member which does not belong.

1 Find a name which describes the
remaining members of the set.

T ={hours, minutes, metres, seconds}
S ={1, 5, 10, 15, 20}
R ={ ⌐, ∧, ∨, ∧, ⌐ }
C ={$\frac{1}{2}$, $\frac{2}{4}$, $\frac{3}{4}$, $\frac{4}{8}$}
O ={ ∨, ⌐, ⌐, ∨, ⌐ }
F ={$\frac{10}{10}$, $\frac{2}{2}$, $\frac{6}{6}$, $\frac{3}{3}$, $\frac{4}{5}$}
P ={ ∕∕, ∖∖, ∖∖, ═, ∕∕ }
M ={cm, mm, kg, m, km}

2 Write the members of each of the
following sets.

Some of the sets have no members,
some have few members and some have
many members.

Use dots where necessary.
X ={days beginning with Z}
H ={children in your family}
E ={even numbers of two figures}
N ={odd numbers greater than 100}
W={multiples of 10 between 101 and 999}
V ={numbers divisible by 3}
Y ={odd numbers between 6 and 8}
Q ={multiples of 8 between 57 and 63}

4, 11, 3, 25, 16, 2, 9, 15, 1, 7

3 Write the members of set A and set B
from the numbers above.
A ={the first 5 square numbers}
B ={the first 5 prime numbers}

4 Write the members of the following sets.
D ={multiples of 2 less than 25}
G ={multiples of 3 less than 25}
J ={multiples of 4 less than 25}
K ={multiples of 6 less than 25}
L ={multiples of 2, 3 and 6 less than 25}
Z ={multiples of 2, 3, 4, 6 less than 25}

Puzzle corner

A

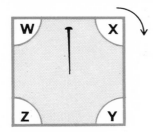

A pin is fixed in the centre of a square card.
The card can be turned round the pin.

1 If the square is turned clockwise so that corner **W** moves to where corner **Z** is now, which corner will **Z** replace?

2 If the first and second letters of the alphabet were changed over and, in the same way, the third and the fourth, the fifth and the sixth and so on, what would then be the twelfth letter of the alphabet?

3 This piece of a metal fence has a mass of 5.6 kg.
If the shaded part is cut off, what will be the mass of the remainder?

Write the two numbers which come next in each of these series.

4 $\frac{1}{4}$	1	$1\frac{3}{4}$	$2\frac{1}{2}$	□	□
5 10	$8\frac{1}{2}$	7	$5\frac{1}{2}$	□	□
6 0.3	0.6	0.9	1.2	□	□
7 0.9	1.8	2.7	3.6	□	□
8 5.6	4.9	4.2	3.5	□	□

In Roman figures:
5 is written V   4 is written IV
6 is written VI   10 is written X.
What do these Roman figures stand for?

9 XIV   **10** XVI   **11** XXI   **12** XXV
13 XXVII   **14** XVIII   **15** XXIV   **16** XIX

B

Look at the pattern. Count the number of:
1 squares   **2** triangles
3 pairs of parallel lines of equal length.

4 Draw a square of 8 cm sides and copy the pattern.

$$\square \times \triangle = 24$$

5 Write numbers in place of □ and △. There are eight different ways of doing this. Write all of them.

6 Divide £1 into TENS and FIVES so that there are twice as many FIVES as TENS. How many of each is that?

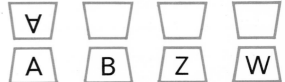

Four letters are written on card and held against a mirror.
7 Draw the reflection that will be seen in the mirror.
The first has been done for you.

If $x=3$ and $y=4$, find the missing number in each of the following.

8 $x+y=\square$ **9** $\frac{y}{x}=\square$ **10** $\frac{\frac{1}{2}x}{y}=\frac{\square}{8}$

11 $y(x)=\square$ **12** $6(y)\div2(x)=\square$

> Look at this example. $167\times38=6346$

Now write the answers only to each of the following.
13 $6346\div38$ **14** $6346\div167$
15 167×380 **16** $(167\times38)\div2$

Number and money addition and subtraction

A Write the answers only. First add upwards. Then check by adding downwards.

1	28 25 +17	2	49 26 +35	3	18 53 +24	4	4.2 3.6 +1.2	5	1.5 3.7 +4.7
6	396 184 +228	7	296 395 +143	8	269 347 +353	9	276 335 +146	10	266 279 +285

Write the answers as £s.

11	53p 19p +12p	12	17p 35p + 8p	13	38p 82p +84p	14	47p 56p +97p	15	57p 94p +88p
16	£ 3·46 4·23 +1·67	17	£ 2·78 1·95 +4·85	18	£ 1·93 3·87 +4·25	19	£ 4·77 4·98 +3·64	20	£ 1·9 7·08 +5·96

Set down the following in vertical columns. Write each answer as £s.

21 £0·79+£4·50+£10·35   22 £11·37+£9·08+£0·36   23 £1·96+58p+£10·63

24 £2·33+£1·77+£12·10   25 £15·80+65p+£8·05   26 £9·59+£8·86+£7·67

B Write the answers only. Check each answer by adding it to the line above.

1	649 −279	2	246 −138	3	578 −229	4	13.5 − 2.6	5	39.5 −17.8
6	683 −164	7	457 −179	8	600 −224	9	91.2 −87.4	10	41.8 −24.3
11	£ 9·83 −2·56	12	£ 8·07 −4·18	13	£ 6·52 −2·03	14	£ 7·46 −2·59	15	£ 15·09 − 6·04
16	£ 13·45 − 9·79	17	£ 21·31 − 7·24	18	£ 11·59 − 8·70	19	£ 38·23 −19·97	20	£ 16·03 −11·58

Set down the following in vertical columns. Write each answer as £s.

21 £7·90−£2·73   22 £15·00−£1·91   23 £11·57−£0·58   24 £8·63−85p

25 £23·67−£12·58   26 £16·55−£13·63   27 £10·24−£5·72   28 £9·10−£4·57

Mark your answers and show the results to your teacher.
There is further addition practice on page 17 and subtraction practice on page 18.

Solids

All the shapes below are **3-D** shapes or solids.

Remember	Shapes which have **length, breadth** and **thickness** and **take up space** are called **solids**.

Get three solids like those shown in the drawings.

Which of the solids is:
1 a cube   **2** a cuboid   **3** a cylinder?

Feel the surfaces of each solid.

Which of the solids:
4 have all flat surfaces
5 has a curved surface?

Examine the solid which is a **cube**.

6 Count the number of edges.
7 How many surfaces has it?
8 Name the shape of each surface.

Place the cube on your desk.
How many of the surfaces are:
9 horizontal   **10** vertical?

Each 'corner' is called a vertex.
'Corners' are called vertices.

11 How many vertices has a cube?

Measure the cube in mm and find its
12 length   **13** breadth   **14** height.
15 Are the measurements the same?

Examine the solid which is a **cuboid**.

16 Count the number of edges.
17 How many surfaces has it?
18 Name the shape of each surface.
19 Are all the surfaces equal in size?

Place the cuboid on your desk.
How many of the surfaces are:
20 horizontal   **21** vertical?
22 How many pairs of opposite equal sides are there?
23 Count the number of vertices on the cuboid.

Examine the solid which is a **cylinder**.

24 Count the number of edges.
25 How many surfaces has it?

How many of the surfaces are:
26 flat   **27** curved?
28 Measure in mm the height, the diameter and the circumference of the cylinder.
29 Make a cylinder without a top and bottom from a rectangular piece of paper.

Get a triangular solid like the one shown in the drawing. Count:
1 the number of edges
2 the number of surfaces.

3 Name the shape of each surface.
4 How many vertices has the solid?

Place the solid on your desk.
How many of the surfaces are:
5 horizontal   **6** vertical   **7** oblique?
8 Measure in mm the length, width and height of the triangular solid.

Solids prisms

A

Ask your teacher to let you examine a packet of writing-paper.

1 The packet is a solid. Name it.
2 Estimate the number of sheets which make up the solid.
3 If fifty of the sheets were used, name the solid which would remain.

Get six Alpha books and put them neatly one on top of the other.

4 You have built a solid. Name it.
5 From the pile take:
   a 3 books   b 5 books.
6 Name the solid which remains in each case.
7 Which of the measurements—the length, the breadth or the height is:
   a the same
   b altered for each of the cuboids?
8 Why is it impossible to build a cube from Alpha books?

B

1 The cream crackers in a packet form a solid. Name it.

There are 30 crackers in the packet.

First, 5 crackers are eaten and then 10 crackers are eaten.

2 Name the solid which remains in each case.

The wrapped loaf is cut into slices.

3 The slices form a solid. Name it.
4 If 3 of the slices are eaten, name the solid which remains.
5 One slice of the loaf is a solid. Name it.
6 Which of the measurements—the length, the breadth or the height is:
   a the same
   b altered for each of the cuboids?

C

Solids which have the same shape and size throughout their length or height and whose sides are parallelograms are called **prisms**.

Which of the cuboids in sections **A** and **B** are   1 square prisms   2 rectangular prisms

3 a Cut out a square of 9 cm side.
   b Using a pencil and a ruler, draw vertical parallel lines 3 cm apart.
   c Fold along the lines and join the two edges with sellotape. You have made a triangular prism.
   d How do you know this solid is a prism?

4 a Cut out a square of 12 cm side.
   b Using a pencil and a ruler, draw horizontal parallel lines 2 cm apart.
   c Fold along the lines and join the two edges with sellotape. You have made a hexagonal prism.
   d How do you know this solid is a prism?

Solids volume

A

| The amount of space a solid takes up is called its **volume**. |

1 cm
1 cm   1 cm

Volume is measured in cubes.
Centimetre cubes are used as the measure for some solids.

1 Get six centimetre cubes and use them to make a square prism.

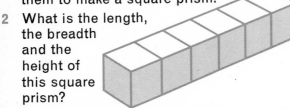

2 What is the length, the breadth and the height of this square prism?

3 What is its volume in centimetre cubes?

4 Now use the six centimetre cubes to make a rectangular prism.

5 What is the length, the breadth and the height of this rectangular prism?

6 What is its volume in centimetre cubes?

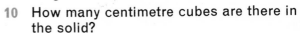
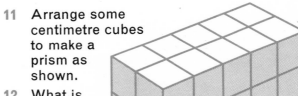

7 Set out a number of centimetre cubes as shown.

8 What is the name of the solid you have made?

9 Find its length, breadth and height.

10 How many centimetre cubes are there in the solid?

11 Arrange some centimetre cubes to make a prism as shown.

12 What is the name of this prism?

13 Write its length, breadth and height.

14 How many centimetre cubes are there?

15 What is the volume of the prism?

B This shape is called a **net**. A box without a lid has been cut along four edges and laid flat.

The net is drawn half size.

1 Using a ruler and a set square, draw the net full size on thin card.

2 Cut out the net and fold along the dotted lines.

3 Stick the edges with sellotape to make the box. It should look like the drawing below.

What is:

4 the length   5 the breadth of the box?

6 How many centimetre cubes will fit on the bottom of the box?

7 What is the height of the box?

8 How many centimetre cubes will the box hold?

9 What is the volume of the box?

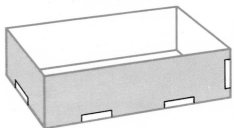

Number and money multiplication and division

A

Write the answers only.

1	2	3	4	5
45 ×5	90 ×6	37 ×8	28 ×4	63 ×7

6	7	8	9	10
360 ×9	452 ×2	158 ×3	109 ×9	247 ×6

11	12	13	14	15
286 ×8	679 ×5	321 ×7	976 ×4	285 ×6

Write the answers first as pence and then as £s.

16	17	18	19	20
48p ×2	27p ×3	19p ×5	23p ×4	16p ×6

Write the answers as £s.

21	22	23	24	25
72p ×7	75p ×9	54p ×8	93p ×6	75p ×2

26	27	28	29	30
£0·07 ×9	£0·24 ×4	£0·18 ×6	£1·03 ×3	£1·60 ×8

31	32	33	34	35
£4·62 ×5	£5·80 ×7	£3·56 ×9	£4·50 ×4	£3·95 ×6

B

Write the answers only.

1	2	3	4	5
2)58	4)96	5)75	3)78	6)84

6	7	8	9	10
7)756	9)135	8)704	4)932	2)910

11	12	13	14	15
3)116	5)924	7)811	9)410	8)845

16	17	18	19	20
6)967	4)837	3)829	7)904	5)444

Write the answers only.

21	22	23	24	25
2)39p	3)88p	4)90p	5)85p	8)92p

26	27	28	29	30
6)£0·39	9)£1·71	7)£5·81	3)£6·81	2)£3·75

31	32	33	34	35
9)£32·13	6)£6·90	8)£30·00	5)£31·15	6)£23·10

Mark your answers and show the results to your teacher.
There is further multiplication practice on page 31 and division practice on page 32.

Surfaces   area

A

1 Move the palm of your hand over:
the top of your desk, a sheet of
writing-paper, the cover of this book,
the seat of your chair.

Feel the amount of surface of each.

Which do you estimate has:

2 the largest   3   the smallest surface?

4 Look at the surface of:
a   the class-room floor   b   the ceiling.

5 What do you know about the amount of
surface of each?

6 Draw and cut out three
squares **X**, **Y** and **Z**.
X side 50 mm
Y side 60 mm
Z side 70 mm

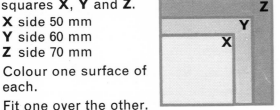

7 Colour one surface of
each.

8 Fit one over the other.

9 Which square has the largest amount of
surface?

10 Draw and cut out two rectangles:
a   7 cm by 4 cm   b   6 cm by 5 cm.

11 Colour one surface of each.

12 Fit one over the other.

13 You cannot compare their areas.

14 Draw and cut out a circle of 25 mm radius.

15 Now draw and cut out
three more circles
making the radius
5 mm larger each time.

16 Colour one surface
of each circle.

17 Fit the circles one
over the other and find which circle has:

a   the largest amount of surface
b   the smallest amount of surface.

> **The amount of surface in a shape
> is called its area.**

18 Why can you compare the areas of
squares and circles by fitting one over
the other, but not rectangles?

B

The rectangles **W**, **X**, **Y** and **Z** are
different in shape.

The surface of each is covered with
squares, all of which are the same size.

1 Which rectangle has the largest area?
How do you know?

2 Which rectangle has the smallest area?
How do you know?

3 Which rectangles have the same area?
How do you know?

On squared paper draw:

4 a square three times the area of **W**

5 a rectangle twice the area of **X**

6 a rectangle of the same area as **Z** but of
a different shape.

C

Squares of the same size have been
used to measure areas.

1 Which of the shapes below could be
used to measure area?

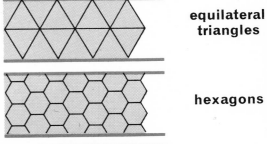

equilateral
triangles

hexagons

circles

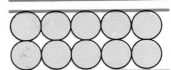

2 Give a reason why:
a   circles cannot be used to measure
areas
b   squares are the most suitable shape
to measure areas.

Surfaces area

A

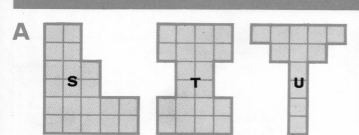

The surface of each of these shapes **S, T, U, V, W** and **X** is covered with squares of equal size.

Look at the shapes **S** and **T**.
1 Are these shapes the same or different?
2 Count the squares in each. What do you find about the area of the shapes?

In the same way, compare the shape and the area of:
3 **U** and **V**   4 **W** and **X**.
What do you find in each case?

On squared paper, draw the following shapes and on each write the number of squares in its area.
5 three different shaped rectangles, each with an area of 24 squares
6 a square and a rectangle, each with an area of 64 squares
7 four different shapes, not rectangles, each of which has an area of 25 squares

Remember Different shapes can have the same area.

B

The area of a shape is measured in equal squares.

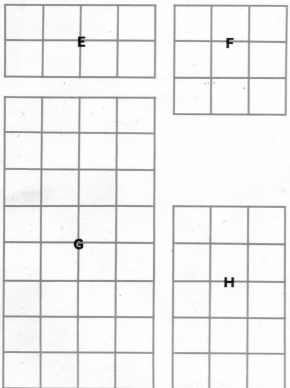

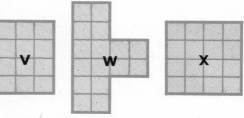

Small areas can be measured in centimetre squares which are written cm².

Look at rectangle **E**. Measure:
1 the length   2 the breadth (width).
3 How many cm² are there in its area?

Write and complete:
4 length of square F = □cm
breadth of square F = □cm
area of square F   = □cm²

5 length of rectangle G = □cm
breadth of rectangle G = □cm
area of rectangle G   = □cm²

6 length of rectangle H = □cm
breadth of rectangle H = □cm
area of rectangle H   = □cm²

7 Find in cm the perimeter of the rectangles **E, G** and **H** and the square **F**.

8 Draw a rectangle which has a length of 6 cm and a perimeter of 16 cm.

Area

A The perimeter of each of the shapes **K** and **L** has been marked off in cm.

K

L

1 Draw this table and complete it.

	shape K	shape L
length	cm	cm
breadth	cm	cm
area	cm²	cm²
perimeter	cm	cm

2 Now check the number of squares in the area by drawing the shapes on cm² squared paper and counting the squares.

The squares can be counted one by one or by a quicker method.

3 Find the quicker method.   **4** Write what you have to do.

B

1 Find the area in cm² of each of the shapes **N**, **O**, **P** and **Q**.

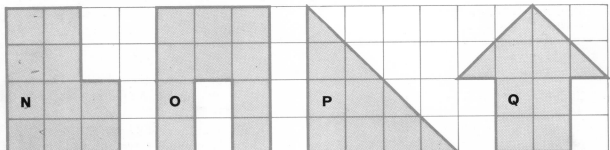

N   **O**   **P**   **Q**

On cm² squared paper draw:

2 a rectangle equal in area to shapes **O** and **Q** together

3 a square equal in area to shapes **P** and **Q** together

4 a rectangle 5 cm long which is equal in area to shapes **N** and **O** together.

C The shape of a leaf is drawn on cm² paper.
To find its approximate area:

1 count the whole squares

2 count as whole squares those which are a half or more. (These have been marked with a dot.) Forget those squares which are less than a half.

3 What is the approximate area in cm² of the leaf?

4 Get a large leaf and draw round it on cm² paper.

5 Find its approximate area in cm².

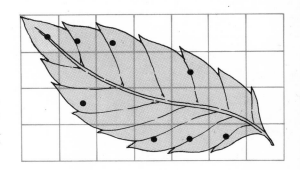

Making sure

A Set down and work these examples.

1	$396+49+2078+500$	6	2750×2	11	635×6	16	$798\div$
2	$88+4627+253+94$	7	1466×3	12	2067×4	17	$1163\div$
3	$3210+38+1746+54$	8	1864×5	13	485×7	18	$4586\div$
4	$5000-2416$	9	583×9	14	740×9	19	$1820\div$
5	$2960-1008$	10	1372×8	15	1080×8	20	$4000\div$

B Write each answer as a decimal.

1	$1+\frac{9}{100}$	7	$4+\frac{39}{100}$	13	$10+\frac{95}{100}$	19	4.52×10	25	3.03×10	31	$10(0.02)$
2	$1+0.01$	8	$3+0.17$	14	$5+0.62$	20	$5.17\text{ m}\times100$	26	$2.08\text{ m}\times100$	32	$100(2.11)$
3	$2+3.55$	9	$7+4.32$	15	$6+2.03$	21	$£0.04\times100$	27	$£0·62\times100$	33	$100(0.48)$
4	$1-\frac{18}{100}$	10	$1-\frac{27}{100}$	16	$1-\frac{54}{100}$	22	$6.5\div10$	28	$138\text{ m}\div10$	34	$\frac{426}{10}$
5	$1-0.04$	11	$1-0.4$	17	$1-0.19$	23	$£505\div100$	29	$90\text{ kg}\div100$	35	$145\ell\div10$
6	$2-1.82$	12	$3-0.07$	18	$4-0.66$	24	$2360\div100$	30	$\frac{1025}{100}$	36	$£\frac{91·00}{100}$

C

This is the flight plan of an air-sea rescue helicopter searching for a missing yacht.

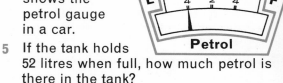

In which direction did the pilot fly:
1 to the search area from the airfield
2 on the first change of course
3 on the second change of course?

4 The pilot returned direct to the airfield from **Y**. In which direction did he fly?

The picture shows the petrol gauge in a car.

5 If the tank holds 52 litres when full, how much petrol is there in the tank?

6 When the pointer is halfway between the $\frac{1}{4}$ and $\frac{1}{2}$ marks, how much petrol is there in the tank?

7 The car travels 8 km per litre. How far will it travel on a full tank?

8 How much petrol will be required for a journey of 320 km?

D

Forest School Fund Collection			
class 1	class 2	class 3	class 4
95p	£1·20	£1·84	£1·37

1 In class 1, one child gave 10p and the remainder 5p each. How many children are there in class 1?

2 Find the total amount saved and divide the answer by 4 to find the average amount saved.

3 Which classes saved above the average?

The empty jar has a mass of 120 g.

4 What is the gross mass of the full jar of marmalade?

5 What is the gross mass, in kg, of 10 jars?

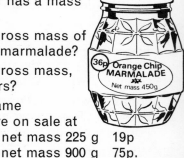

Jars of the same marmalade are on sale at these prices: net mass 225 g 19p
net mass 900 g 75p.

6 Which of the **three** sizes gives the best value for money?

Decimals notation + − × ÷

A

Write as decimals.

1. $35\frac{6}{10}$ 2. $2\frac{2}{10}$ 3. $100\frac{4}{10}$ 4. $135\frac{2}{10}$

Multiply by 10.

5. 5   6. 0.5   7. 18   8. 1.8

9. 0.7   10. 70   11. 21.6   12. 20.7

Divide by 10.

13. 40   14. 4   15. 560   16. 56

17. 19   18. 273   19. 390   20. 11

Write and complete:

21. 9.6   =   □units □tenths   =   □tenths

22. 7.3   =   □units □tenths   =   □tenths

23. 11.5   =   □ten □unit □tenths
              =   □units □tenths   =   □tenths

24. 20.4   =   □tens □units □tenths
              =   □units □tenths   =   □tenths

25. 362.9   =   □hundreds □tens □units □tenths
              =   □tens □units □tenths
              =   □units □tenths   =   □tenths.

Write and complete:

26. 90 tenths   =   □units

27. 45 tenths   =   □units □tenths

28. 126 tenths   =   □units □tenths
                 =   □ten □units □tenths

29. 205 tenths   =   □units □tenths
                 =   □tens □units □tenths

30. 377 tenths   =   □units □tenths
                 =   □tens □units □tenths.

B

Write as decimals.

1. 9 hundredths   2. 7 hundredths   3. $\frac{1}{100}$

4. $\frac{6}{100}$ 5. $\frac{2}{100}$ 6. $\frac{4}{100}$

Multiply by 10.

7. 0.8   8. 0.08   9. 1.9   10. 0.19

11. 2.56   12. 10.13   13. 28.75   14. 80.05

Divide by 10.

15. 0.2   16. 0.6   17. 1.1   18. 5.7

19. 14.3   20. 10.4   21. 36.8   22. 100.5

Write and complete:

23. 0.54   =   □tenths □hundredths
            =   □hundredths

24. 1.83   =   □unit □tenths □hundredths
            =   □tenths □hundredths
            =   □hundredths

25. 7.65   =   □ $+\frac{□}{10}+\frac{□}{100}$

26. 8.07   = $8+\frac{□}{100}$

27. 28.55   = $20+8+\frac{□}{10}+\frac{□}{100}$

28. 46.32   = $40+6+\frac{□}{10}+\frac{□}{100}$ = $\frac{□}{100}$.

Write as decimals.

29. 359 hundredths   30. 792 hundredths

31. 506 hundredths   32. 860 hundredths

33. $\frac{835}{100}$ 34. $\frac{1166}{100}$ 35. $\frac{1004}{100}$

Change the following to vulgar fractions in their lowest terms.

36. 0.5   37. 0.75   38. 0.25

39. 0.04   40. 0.35   41. 0.65

C

Write the answers only.

1. 7−0.5   2. 2−0.2   3. 10−0.6

4. 5.1−0.3   5. 2.8−0.9   6. 3.3−1.7

7. 0.6+0.9   8. 3.7+1.4   9. 4.5+4.5

10. 2.8+1.7   11. 2.2+3.9   12. 10.6+8.4

Multiply by 10.

13. £1·86   14. 6.4 cm   15. 8.2 m

16. 0.75 km   17. 0.25 kg   18. 0.5 ℓ

19. 5.36 m   20. £2·10   21. 1.3 kg

Divide by 10.

22. £6·70   23. 95 cm   24. 23 m

25. 41 km   26. 8 kg   27. 79 ℓ

28. £15·00   29. 3 km   30. 5.5 m

Write the answers only.

31. 1−0.05   32. 1−0.35   33. 1−0.75

34. 4−0.62   35. 5−0.87   36. 10−0.99

37. 0.62+0.38   38. 0.15+0.25   39. 0.41+0.3

40. 0.95+0.06   41. 0.57+0.52   42. 0.2+0.18

Multiply by 100.

43. £2·42   44. 3.65 m   45. 1.75 kg

46. 0.5 cm   47. 2.25 km   48. 3.6 ℓ

49. £4·10   50. 1.7 kg   51. 0.37 m

Divide by 100.

52. £27·00   53. 59 m   54. 110 cm

55. 4 km   56. 15 kg   57. 27 ℓ

58. £106   59. 122 kg   60. 130 ℓ

Puzzle corner

A

1 A boy rides his bicycle so that his distance from a post is always 30 metres. Draw a plan to show the post and the track to a scale of 1 cm to 10 m.

2 Find the number nearest to 101 which will have a remainder of 2 when divided by 7.

3 12 posts are set in a row, each one $2\frac{1}{2}$ metres from the next. How far is it from the first to the last post?

4 Share a FIFTY and a TEN among Joan, Tony and Pat so that Joan has 5p more than Tony and Tony has 5p more than Pat.

5 Find the value of x when $x+5=2x-5$.

6 Which number when multiplied by itself has a product of:
   a 64   b 81   c 121?

B
Draw what should come next in each of the rows.

1 **2** **3**

4 **5** **6**

C

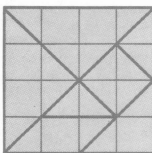

This is an old Chinese puzzle called a **tangram**.

1 a On thin card, draw and cut out a square of 4 cm side.
  b Rule the square into 16 equal squares as shown.
  c Copy the tangram carefully and cut out the seven pieces.

How many of the pieces are:
2 squares   **3** triangles   **4** parallelograms?
5 Mix up the pieces and then, without looking at the diagram, fit them together again to make the square.

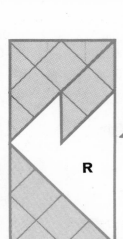
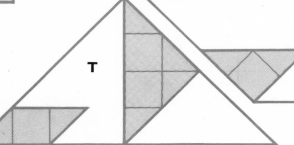

Some pieces of the tangram have been used in shapes **R**, **T** and **P**.

6 Set out the pieces as shown in the rectangle and then complete it.
In the same way, first set out and then complete:
7 the triangle   **8** the parallelogram.
9 What do you know about the area of the four shapes?
10 Use the tangram to make several interesting shapes.

Plans drawing to scale

Plans show the shape of objects when looked at from above.

A

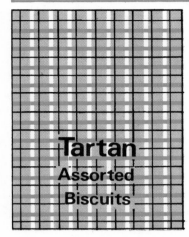

Tartan
Assorted
Biscuits

A box of biscuits has been placed flat on a table and the drawing shows how it looks from above.

It is a **plan** of the box.
The plan has been drawn a quarter of the actual size.

1 Find from the plan the actual length and width of the box.

2 Use a ruler and a set square to draw the plan half the actual size.

3 Which measurement is not shown on the plan?

4 The height of the box is 6 cm. Imagine the box is standing on one end. Draw a plan half size in this position.

5 Imagine the box is standing on one side. Draw a plan half size in this position.

B Using a ruler, compasses and a set square, draw a plan half size of each of these objects.

Show the measurements on each plan.

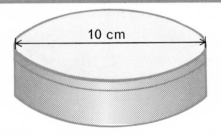

10 cm

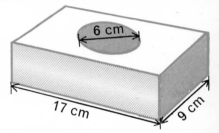

6 cm

17 cm   9 cm

C

plan of box

The drawing is the plan of another box.
It has been drawn $\frac{1}{5}$ of the actual size.

1 Measure   a in cm   b in mm
the length and width of the box on the plan.

2 Find the actual length and width of the box   a in cm   b in mm.

Write and complete:

3 The plan has been drawn to the scale 1 cm to ☐ cm or 1 mm to ☐ mm.

4 If the plan had been drawn to the scale of 1 cm to 10 cm, write this scale in mm, i.e. 1 mm to ☐ mm.

5 Using this scale, what fraction of the actual measurements are the measurements on the plan?

6 Find the actual length and width of the box.

D Find the actual length represented by each of these lines.

1 ———————————— Scale 1 mm to 5 mm

2 ————————————— Scale 1 cm to 4 cm

3 ——————— Scale 1 cm to 10 cm

4 —————————————— Scale 1 mm to 10 mm

5 ——————————— Scale 1 mm to 100 mm

Plans drawing to scale

A

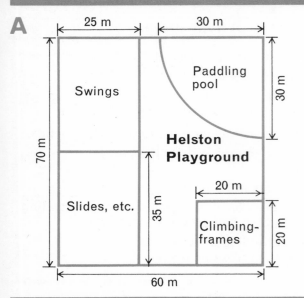

The drawing shows the size and layout of a children's playground.

Write in metres:

1 the length   2 the width of the playground.

3 Using a ruler and a set square, draw a plan of the playground to the scale 1 cm to 10 metres.

4 Find the total distance in metres round the whole playground.

Find the perimeter of:

5 the climbing-frame area

6 the swings area

7 the area for slides, etc.

8 What fraction of a circle is the paddling pool?

9 What is the name of its shape?

B

This is a plan of a small park with the main pathways shown.

In which direction does Peter turn, right or left, if he walks by the paths from:

1 Gate A to Gate F   2 Gate B to Gate C   3 Gate D to Gate F   4 Gate E to Gate C?

Which of the gates could be called:

5 North Gate   6 South Gate

7 East Gate   8 West Gate?

9 Draw and complete this table. (When measuring the roads, measure the side nearer to the park.)

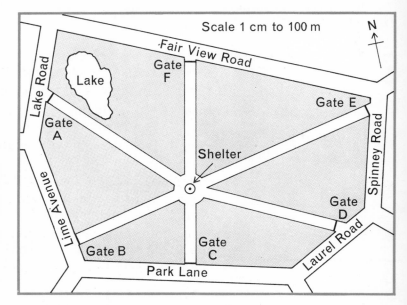

	length on plan	actual length
Fair View Road		
Lake Road		
Lime Avenue		
Park Lane		
Laurel Road		
Spinney Road		

10 Find in cm the perimeter of the park on the plan.

11 What is the distance round the park in metres?

12 How many metres less than 3 km is that?

Find the actual distances along these paths:

13 from gate B to gate E   14 from gate F to gate C.

There is a shelter where the paths meet.

15 Find the distance in m from the shelter to gate D   to gate A.

16 Find the greatest length of the lake in metres.

Plans drawing to scale

Maps are plans.
The scale of a map is always given so that actual distances can be found by measuring.

A

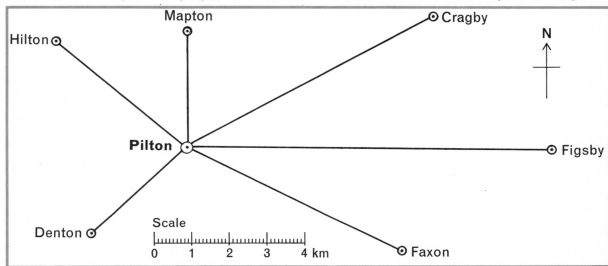

The map shows the town called Pilton and six nearby villages.

1 Measure the scale shown on the map and then write it in this way: 1 cm to ☐ km.

2 What decimal fraction of 1 km is represented by 1 mm?

3 Write: The scale is 1 mm to ☐ km.

4 Find, by measuring in mm on the plan and using the scale, the actual distance from Pilton to each of the villages.

Find the actual distance in km 'as the crow flies' from:

5 Faxon to Mapton   6 Denton to Figsby

7 Hilton to Cragby   8 Figsby to Faxon.

9 Which village is north of Pilton?
Find the approximate direction from Pilton to:

10 Figsby   11 Denton   12 Faxon

13 Cragby   14 Hilton.

15 If the map had been drawn using the scale below, what would 1 cm represent?

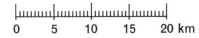

16 What would 1 mm represent?

17 Write: The scale is 1 mm to ☐ km.

18 Using this scale, find the distance from Pilton to each of the villages.

B Using the scale:

1 1 cm to 100 m, draw lines to represent
a 300 m   b 750 m   c 1.4 km

2 1 cm to 200 m, draw lines to represent
a 600 m   b 900 m   c 1.5 km

3 1 cm to 500 m, draw lines to represent
a 2 km   b 3 km   c 5.5 km

4 1 cm to 1 km, draw lines to represent
a 10 km   b 13.5 km   c 8.3 km

5 1 cm to 10 km, draw lines to represent
a 40 km   b 85 km   c 115 km.

Measure these lines carefully and then find the scale to which each line is drawn.

The length each represents is given.

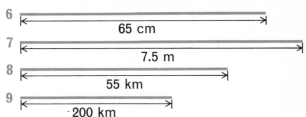

6 65 cm

7 7.5 m

8 55 km

9 200 km

Making sure

A How many g less than 1 kg is:
1 826 g   2 648 g   3 905 g
4 763 g   5 928 g   6 877 g?

How many g less than ½ kg is:
7 464 g   8 339 g   9 295 g
10 354 g   11 188 g   12 462 g?

Write as a decimal fraction of 1 kg.
13 400 g   14 800 g   15 700 g
16 500 g   17 200 g   18 900 g

How many g are there in:
19 4.1 kg   20 6.3 kg   21 2.6 kg?

Write as kg.
22 5180 g   23 4110 g   24 3760 g

How many g are there in:
25 2.166 kg   26 5.099 kg   27 4.370 kg?

How many m in:
28 ½ km   29 ¼ km   30 ¾ km?

How many mℓ less than 1 ℓ is:
31 851 mℓ   32 590 mℓ   33 715 mℓ?

How many mℓ more than ½ ℓ is:
34 582 mℓ   35 618 mℓ   36 769 mℓ?

Write as a decimal fraction of 1 ℓ.
37 100 mℓ   38 500 mℓ   39 200 mℓ

How many mm more than 1 m is:
40 1075 mm   41 1062 mm   42 1182 mm?

How many mm less than ½ m is:
43 279 mm   44 410 mm   45 364 mm?

Write as a decimal fraction of 1 m.
46 700 mm   47 600 mm   48 300 mm

Write as m.
49 4380 mm   50 7245 mm   51 1962 mm

How many mm are there in:
52 4.175 m   53 2.210 m   54 3.295 m?

B Write to the nearest m.
1 390 cm   2 546 cm   3 718 cm
4 6280 mm   5 4875 mm   6 6500 mm

Write to the nearest ½ m.
7 460 cm   8 385 cm   9 219 cm
10 3600 mm   11 8400 mm   12 1180 mm

Write to the nearest cm.
13 118 mm   14 72 mm   15 350 mm
16 36.3 cm   17 24.9 cm   18 15.5 cm

Write to the nearest km.
19 7820 m   20 5650 m   21 9270 m

Write to the nearest ½ km.
22 4620 m   23 3200 m   24 5800 m

Write to the nearest kg.
25 2090 g   26 7670 g   27 5150 g
28 4065 g   29 3920 g   30 6610 g

Write to the nearest ½ kg.
31 4150 g   32 6710 g   33 3400 g

C Write the value of the figure underlined in each of these numbers.
1 29.5   2 80.04   3 7435.2   4 1069.7   5 123.87   6 132.65

Write the value of the figure underlined in each of these sums of money.
7 £246·70   8 £20·15   9 £1428·00   10 £93·84   11 £45·60   12 £372·19

| Multiply by 10 | 13 2.48 | 14 18.7 | 15 £2·06 | 16 £0·31 |
| Multiply by 100 | 17 5.23 | 18 80.9 | 19 £0·56 | 20 £7·03 |

| Divide by 10 | 21 8004 | 22 28.6 | 23 £20·70 | 24 £45·00 |
| Divide by 100 | 25 580 | 26 611 | 27 £22·00 | 28 £9·00 |

Change the following to hundredths. Then write them as decimal fractions.
29 $\frac{3}{4}$ 30 $\frac{1}{20}$ 31 $\frac{7}{20}$ 32 $\frac{19}{50}$ 33 $\frac{6}{25}$ 34 $\frac{18}{25}$

Change the following to vulgar fractions in their lowest terms.
35 0.45   36 0.64   37 0.12   38 0.55   39 0.88   40 0.15

Making sure

A

1. Write the months of the year in order.
2. Against the months, write the number of days in each.
3. How many days in February in a leap year?
4. Write this date, using figures only. the twentieth of August nineteen eighty-four

Write and complete:

5. $1 \text{ min} = \square \text{s}$ 6. $\frac{1}{2} \text{ min} = \square \text{s}$ 7. $\frac{1}{4} \text{ min} = \square \text{s}$
8. $\frac{3}{4} \text{ min} = \square \text{s}$ 9. $1 \text{ h} = \square \text{min}$ 10. $\frac{1}{2} \text{ h} = \square \text{min}$
11. $\frac{1}{4} \text{ h} = \square \text{min}$ 12. $\frac{3}{4} \text{ h} = \square \text{min}$ 13. $1 \text{ day} = \square \text{h}$
14. $1 \text{ week} = \square \text{days}$ 15. $1 \text{ year} = \square \text{weeks}$
16. $1 \text{ year} = \square \text{days}$ 17. $1 \text{ year} = \square \text{months}$.

B

1. The temperature reading on a thermometer is **15°C**. What does the '°C' stand for?
2. At what temperature does   a   water freeze   b   water boil?
3. Estimate the temperature to which your class-room is usually heated.

Find the difference in degrees C between:

4. 9°C and 15°C   5. 22°C and 14°C   6. −8°C and −3°C   7. −1°C and −6°C
8. −10°C and 0°C   9. 4°C and −1°C   10. 2°C and −7°C   11. −5°C and 4°C.

C

Which measure or measures would you usually ask for if you wished to buy:

1. potatoes   2. petrol   3. paint   4. wood   5. carpets
6. clothing   7. writing-paper   8. sweets   9. milk   10. biscuits?

In each of the following, six measurements are given.
Choose for the answer the measurement which you think is the best estimate.

11	the height of a man	100 cm	125 cm	130 cm	145 cm	185 cm	250 cm
12	the length of a bed	100 cm	200 cm	300 cm	350 cm	400 cm	450 cm
13	the length of this page	900 mm	700 mm	600 mm	450 mm	250 mm	100 mm
14	a bottle of milk	250 mℓ	500 mℓ	1 litre	1.5 ℓ	2 ℓ	2.5 ℓ
15	a large packet of flour	150 g	375 g	575 g	1.5 kg	3 kg	5 kg
16	a large bottle of orangeade	$\frac{1}{4}$ ℓ	1 ℓ	2 ℓ	3 ℓ	5 ℓ	7 ℓ
17	the height of teacher's desk	300 mm	350 mm	500 mm	750 mm	1000 mm	1500 mm

D

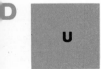 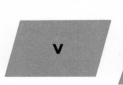   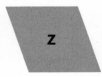

1. Name each of the shapes.
2. Measure in mm   a   the diameter   b   the radius of shape **X**.
3. Measure to the nearest $\frac{1}{2}$ cm a diagonal of   a   the square   b   the rectangle.
4. By how many mm is one diagonal longer than the other in   a   shape **V**   b   shape **Z**?
5. Find in mm the length of the perimeter of each of the shapes **U, V, W, Y** and **Z**.

Making sure

A **Turn to page 12 and test yourself on the addition and subtraction facts.**

$$\frac{12}{16} \qquad \frac{4}{8} \qquad \frac{5}{10} \qquad \frac{9}{12}$$
$$\frac{5}{20} \qquad \frac{3}{6} \qquad \frac{2}{8} \qquad \frac{75}{100} \qquad \frac{25}{100}$$

1 From the fractions in the box write the following sets.
W = {three fractions each equal to $\frac{1}{2}$}
X = {three fractions each equal to $\frac{1}{4}$}
Y = {three fractions each equal to $\frac{3}{4}$}

Write each of the following to the nearest whole one.
2 $\frac{9}{4}$ 3 $11\frac{7}{8}$ 4 $24\frac{1}{12}$ 5 $17\frac{3}{7}$
6 28.39 7 39.7 8 46.18 9 22.51

10 Jane spent $\frac{1}{3}$ of her savings on gifts and $\frac{1}{2}$ on books. What fraction remains?

Write in 24-hour clock times.
11 8.00 a.m. 12 1.00 a.m. 13 2.37 a.m
14 4.00 p.m. 15 10.30 p.m. 16 5.53 p.m.
17 9.16 p.m. 18 3.35 p.m. 19 9.08 p.m

Write in 12-hour clock times.
20 11.00 21 20.00 22 13.00
23 04.30 24 18.15 25 15.45
26 23.20 27 19.16 28 23.59

How many h and min from:
29 09.50 to 11.45   30 00.00 to 01.20
31 04.38 to 06.00   32 16.45 to 17.58?

How many h and min from:
33 5.23 p.m. to 7.00 p.m.
34 10.40 p.m. to midnight
35 2.15 a.m. to 3.10 a.m.
36 11.15 a.m. to 12.40 p.m?

B Draw triangles with these measurements.
1 **T** 55 mm 35 mm 45 mm   2 **U** 35 mm 60 mm 60 mm   3 **V** 45 mm 60 mm 75 mm
4 **W** 40 mm 50 mm 80 mm   5 **X** 55 mm 55 mm 55 mm   6 **Y** 50 mm 40 mm 50 mm
7 Name each triangle according to its sides: scalene, isosceles or equilateral.
8 Name each triangle according to its angles: right-angled, obtuse-angled or acute-angled.
9 Which of the triangles are symmetrical?

How many degrees are there in:
10 one complete turn   11 a straight angle   12 the three angles of a triangle?

13 Find the number of degrees in the angles marked **k, l, m** and **n**.

These distances were recorded on a journey by car.
Find the distance in km from:
14 Kettering to Harwich   15 Huntingdon to Colchester   16 Cambridge to Harwich
17 Colchester to Harwich.
18 Draw the diagram to a scale of 1 cm to 10 km. Mark and name each town.

Making sure

A **Turn to page 25 and test yourself on the multiplication and division facts.**

The solids **D** and **E** have been made with centimetre cubes. Remember that each edge of a centimetre cube measures 1 cm.

1 Find the length, breadth and height of solid **D**, solid **E**.

2 Which of the solids is:
a a cube
b a cuboid or rectangular prism?

3 How do you know?

4 How many centimetre cubes are there in solid **D**, solid **E**?

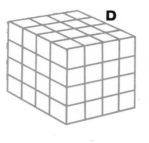
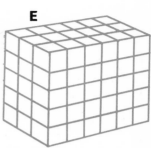

5 Measure in mm the length and breadth of this rectangle.

6 How many 5 mm squares would be needed to cover its surface?

7 Find the perimeter in mm.

8 Find the area in cm².

9 Draw a circle of 25 mm radius. Use a ruler and a 45° set square to draw pattern **F**.

10 Draw a circle of 3.5 cm radius. Use a ruler and compasses only to draw pattern **G**.

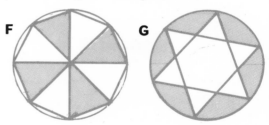

B Write answers only to these examples. Work as quickly as you can.

Write the value of each figure underlined.

1 317.<u>9</u>   2 2.<u>0</u>4   3 10<u>4</u>0.6<u>8</u>

How much greater in value is £1·00 than:

4 7 TENS   5 18 FIVES   6 26 TWOS?

7 17.04×10 8 0.32×100

9 $\frac{2}{3}$ of 2.64 m. Write the answer in cm.

10 A man walks 6 km in an hour.
How long will it take him to walk 9 km?

11 Which of these fractions is:
a the greatest   b the least?
$\frac{1}{2}$ $\frac{3}{8}$ $\frac{2}{3}$ $\frac{1}{4}$

12 How many picture cards at 9p each can be bought for a FIFTY?

13 David has 25p and James has 3 times as much. How much have they altogether?

14 A box, when full, has a mass of 2.3 kg.
The mass of the box is $\frac{1}{2}$ kg.
Find the mass of the contents of the box.

15 Tom has 47 marbles and John has 25.
How many must Tom give to John so that each has an equal number?

16 4 runners in a relay team each run 400 metres. Find in km the total distance the team runs.

Find the average of:

17 4 km   7 km   5 km   6 km   8 km

18 50 cm   80 cm   70 cm   40 cm

19 £2·50   £4·00   £2·65.

20 98p was paid with four silver coins and three copper coins. Name them.

21 $18 = y + y$ $y \times y = 81$
Find the value of 6 times y.

22 A square and an equilateral triangle each has a perimeter of 36 cm. Find the length of one side of each shape.

23 $y - z = 3$ $y \times z = 54$
Find the value of y, of z.

Making sure

A

2	3	4	5	6	7	8	9	10	11	12	13	14	15	16
17	18	19	20	21	22	23	24	25	26	27	28	29	30	31

1 Using the numbers in the box only, write and complete these sets.

O = {odd numbers}   Z = {even numbers}   P = {prime numbers}
T = {multiples of 2}   H = {multiples of 3}   N = {multiples of 9}
F = {multiples of 4}   G = {multiples of 6}   E = {multiples of 8}
K = {multiples of both 2 and 5}   L = {multiples of 2, 3 and 6}   M = {multiples of 4, 6 and 8}

Find the value of y in each of the following.

2 $(2 \times 4) + 3 = y$ 3 $(3 \times 6) - 8 = y$ 4 $(32 \div 4) + 5 = y$ 5 $y + (3 \times 8) = 2$

6 $(40 \div 8) - y = 3$ 7 $(y \times 2) + 1 = 5$ 8 $2(y) + 7 = 25$ 9 $y^2 - 4 = 60$

10 $\dfrac{25}{y} = y$ 11 $\dfrac{y}{4} = 7$ 12 $\dfrac{y + y + y + y}{2} = 16$ 13 $y(7 + 2) = 54$

B

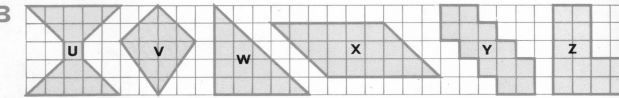

1 Copy the shapes on a sheet of squared paper.
2 Cut them out and, by folding, find the shapes which have:
   a one line of symmetry   b two lines of symmetry   c no line of symmetr

The pictures of these mini toys are drawn to the scale 1 mm to 5 mm.
Find the actual length of each toy.

Find the actual length, in metres, represented by each of these lines.

6 ———————————————————————————— Scale 1 mm to 10 cm
7 ———————————————————————————— Scale 1 cm to 10 cm
8 —————————————————————— Scale 1 mm to 1 m
9 ———————————————————— Scale 1 cm to 5 cm

C

Shilton School Penny Fund			
week ending	class 1	class 2	class 3
2 March	23p	30p	27p
9 March	37p	19p	53p
16 March	18p	36p	46p
23 March	45p	24p	14p

The table shows the number of pennies collected in each class.

1 Find in £s the total collected:
   a by each class
   b by the school during each week
   c by the school during the four weeks

2 Find a method of checking the grand total.